# Manthology

# Manthology

[ POEMS ON THE MALE EXPERIENCE ]

Edited by Craig Crist-Evans,
Kate Fetherston, and
Roger Weingarten

UNIVERSITY OF IOWA PRESS | IOWA CITY

University of Iowa Press, Iowa City 52242

Copyright © 2006 by the University of Iowa Press

http://www.uiowa.edu/uiowapress

Design by April Leidig-Higgins

The University of Iowa Press is a member of Green
Press Initiative and is committed to preserving natural
resources.

Printed on acid-free paper

Library of Congress Cataloging-in-Publication Data
Manthology: poems on the male experience / edited by
Craig Crist-Evans, Kate Fetherston, and Roger Weingarten.
     p.   cm.
Includes index.
ISBN 0-87745-988-6 (pbk.)
1. Men — Poetry.   2. American poetry — 21st century.
I. Crist-Evans, Craig.   II. Fetherston, Kate.
III. Weingarten, Roger.
PS595.M46 M36   2006
811'.608/03521 22                    2005056886

06  07  08  09  10  P  5  4  3  2  1

for Craig Crist-Evans
1954–2005

# Contents

# Introduction

WHY FOCUS AN ANTHOLOGY of poems on the male experience when, for centuries, men have pretty much dominated everything from politics to the literary canon? Hasn't everything that *can* be said about the male experience already *been* said? We found out by editing this collection that the answer is a resounding *no*. As Christopher Buckley's poem "Catechism of the Sea" suggests:

> Pick any five men
> mumbling in their coats, drifting
>
> On the cliff-side benches, an on-shore breeze
> at their unmetaphysical throats
>
> And see how many words of allegiance or joy
> can be squeezed out at this late date.

In *Manthology*, ninety-three poets offer their words of allegiance, joy, love, hate, anger, shame, alienation, guilt, and a full spectrum of other responses to the male experience. In tones ranging from serious to humorous, ponderous to flippant, funereal to frenetic, poets such as Marvin Bell, Robert Bly, Mark Doty, Stephen Dunn, Stuart Dybek, Ray González, Tony Hoagland, Jonathan Holden, Richard Howard, Sydney Lea, Philip Levine, Jack Myers, Tim Seibles, Arthur Sze, Charles Harper Webb, and David Wojahn render poetic descriptions of events and emotions in the lives of boys and men. You will also notice poems by women the three of us saw as essential to this collection: Rita Dove, Alice Fulton, Jane Hirshfield, Naomi Shihab Nye, Clare Rossini, Maureen Seaton, and Dara Wier among them. You have only to read their poems to acknowledge that these gifted poets—in their roles as sisters, girlfriends, wives, lovers, and mothers—have closely, with inventive language and formal range, observed the boys and men in their lives. Try reading Sharon Doubiago's "How to Make Love to a Man," Lynn Emanuel's "Walt, I Salute You!" Elinor Benedict's "At Ease," Stefi Weisburd's "Sponge Boy," or Victoria Redel's "Bedecked."

WHAT KIND OF MAN is represented in *Manthology*? Every man you've ever known: your father, your brother, your grandfather, your uncle, your son, your husband, your lover, your self. Also personified on these pages are the strangers whose lives you may have glimpsed but not known: a drug addict ("In the Park" by Tom Sleigh), a victim of street-gang violence ("Pulp Fiction" by David Baker), a soldier ("The Uniform" by Marvin Bell), an African child mutilated in a civil war ("The Calling" by Ai), a mugger ("Prayer for the Man Who Mugged My Father, 72" by Charles Harper Webb).

We received, in response to our call for submissions, many poems you would expect to find in a book chronicling the male experience. Poems about sports, such as Gary Margolis's "Lacrosse"; poems about blue-collar work and play, such as Marcus Cafagña's "Hawthorne Metal, Detroit, 1939" or Jonathan Holden's "The Men in the Hoboken Bar"; poems about the military, such as David Wojahn's "Wartime Photos of My Father"; poems about the father/son relationship, such as Robert Alexander's "For Years My Father" or Robert Bly's "When My Dead Father Called"; and of course the many poems about sexual initiation or conquest, such as Christopher Bursk's "What a Boy Does Not Say," Mark Halliday's "Questmale," or Tony Hoagland's "Dickhead."

We also received poems of great tenderness and introspection: "A man filled with the gladness of living" in Richard Tillinghast's "Table," places "flowers in a copper bowl there." Greg Delanty's "The Goat" describes being haunted by the futility of "reaching to help hurt creatures" that "usually react in fear." Kevin Stein's "Terms" at first appears to be another poem about drinking and partying, but acknowledges "we're drinking / like this because we want a child and we can't / have one." And the twelve-year-old boy in Stephen Dunn's "The Routine Things around the House" acknowledges that his mother's allowing him a glimpse of her breasts is the reason he is able "to love women easily."

Your challenge, as you read *Manthology*, is to follow the advice that Billy Collins gave us after reviewing the poems we had chosen from the ones he sent us. "The idea isn't so much that the poems celebrate men as that they challenge the reader to discover for him or herself what is male about the poem."

# Manthology

# The Calling

I promised I'd be good that day
and go to missionary school,
but the bad man still came to punish me.
My mother begged him to spare my life,
but he said, "woman, I am Africa
and Africa takes what it wants."
He opened a box and she looked inside,
then she screamed and fell to her knees.
Before I knew what was happening,
pain shot a fiery bullet into my arm.
When I came to, I was surprised
for my whole body told me I died
when death shook my hand.
My mother burned the stump to cauterize it.
Is healing agony? It must be, I decided,
as I lay in the strange quiet of morning.
Not even a cock crowed,
no women went to get water for cooking,
no scent of plantains and stew
blew into our hut.
I shut my eyes and tried to ride
the waves of nausea
flowing through my body
to someplace where suffering did not exist,
but it was useless.
Again and again, I returned to the place
where my hand, clenched in a fist
lay in a box with other hands
in various states of decay.
When my mother shook me awake,
I knew what I would do.
"Get me a knife," I told her.

I began to practice slicing melons
with one hand,
until I could take my place
beside the man who's like a father to me now,
as we wander around, demanding reparations
in pounds of flesh.
In the villages, they call me "The Chopper,"
and they say it with respect.

# For Years My Father

For years my father practiced the violin: "What d'ya think, Rob, am I wasting my time sawing away on this hunk of wood?" I would lie on the couch listening to him, New York receding behind the glass panes of the living room. My mother of course had to listen to him play more than I, but she too found it a pleasure, not so much from enjoyment of the sound as from what the sound suggested of the pleasure he was having. Often he said that it was his meditation—trying to play in tune, keep the bow balanced and light—and when he died, at home, he had just finished playing Beethoven's Spring Sonata with his brother Josef. My aunt and uncle had come over for dinner, and after dinner my aunt is talking to my mother—who is keeping rather silent, I think—and my father and my uncle are playing. When they finish the last movement of the Spring Sonata my mother asks my father if he doesn't think it's time to stop, and he smiles and says Yes and dies in the chair where he's sitting, violin and bow still in his hands. Later my uncle tells me that while my father plays, "It's as though he's never been sick."

# The Vigil

Look again . . . the fence glistening in overcast light, the grass at its brightest. Images of no one. Of
    one's own family, burying itself. Rust-colored earth, or it seemed that way—I don't
    remember.

Old fool, the mask is inside—no one sees through you but me. And it's winter and pacing, the
    conversations you'll have, and the person you speak to agrees.

But listen. Listen . . . how the living cry out in their cars, in the stillness of sleep. The lover left out—
    pure harmony!

My love in the kitchen, paring apples—and why not? Why shouldn't she? The marvel of her
    hands, her head tilted that way. Humming to herself, or dreaming, smiling when she sees
    me—

what am I that your spirit's a killer!

# Pulp Fiction

*You want more? You want some more of* this shit?
so he puts his weight to his elbow jammed
under the jaw of the other one pinned
there, panicked, panting, his back to the bricks.
The others are loud and jeering and stand
in a jackal circle a spitting-length
away. The cold air is full of bird song.

The sex—sheer sugar—of the flowering trees
turns to powder against the skin, and cakes
the sidewalks pale green, and packs the curbs.
Far away a powerful siren cries.
Someone is about to get his ass kicked.
But now the cruel gang spots someone—okay,
it's me—who is writing this whole scene down.

It's so easy to surpass the limits
of the powers of description. *What are*
*you looking at?* There are yellow flowers
sprouting from the downspout above their heads.
The powers of discursion are no less
feeble, frail as the least petal. *Stop it!*
They don't stop it. The one in trouble is

starting to weep, and the others to laugh,
as the one with the elbow suddenly
slips a white-handled knife from his pocket.
(Is this the big city? Are there dime bags
dropping from the claws of carrion birds?
Have his bad colors taunted the wrong turf?)
No. No. No. This is just my little town,

and the hostile gang is as easily
eight years old as twenty, out of grade school
since three o'clock. I'm sorry for my mind,
but the spring has spread a violent seed
and it has taken root in this poem,
as in my heart, in the children beating
each other to a pulp in your city

as well as mine. Is it less barbarous
to turn now toward the beautiful? Once
there was a hillside of white, wild lilies.
The mayapples were spilling there. A first
green froth of spring ferns spread under the pines —
so the pastoral, unperturbed lilies
stand around our absence in the sunlight.

What have we done to deserve the pollen,
the plant persistence, of our natures? You
want more? The boys beat the daylights out of
the poor boy and I do nothing to help.
And the flowers are fiction — descriptive,
discursive — designed to suggest my mind
in peace or shame. So are the boys, if

the truth be told. So are the sexual trees.
The knife, you understand, is real. The knife is mine.

# The Uniform

Of the sleeves, I remember their weight, like wet wool,
on my arms, and the empty ends which hung past my hands.
Of the body of the shirt, I remember the large buttons
and larger buttonholes, which made a rack of wheels
down my chest and could not be quickly unbuttoned.
Of the collar, I remember its thickness without starch,
by which it lay against my clavicle without moving.
Of my trousers, the same—heavy, bulky, slow to give
for a leg, a crowded feeling, a molasses to walk in.
Of my boots, I remember the brittle soles, of a material
that had not been made love to by any natural substance,
and the laces: ropes to make prisoners of my feet.
Of the helmet, I remember the webbed, inner liner,
a brittle plastic underwear on which wobbled
the crushing steel pot then strapped at the chin.
Of the mortar, I remember the mortar plate,
heavy enough to kill by weight, which I carried by rope.
Of the machine gun, I remember the way it fit
behind my head and across my shoulder blades
as I carried it, or, to be precise, as it rode me.
Of tactics, I remember the likelihood of shooting
the wrong man, the weight of the rifle bolt, the difficulty
of loading while prone, the shock of noise.
For earplugs, some used cigarette filters or toilet paper.
I don't hear well now, for a man of my age,
and the doctor says my ears were damaged and asks
if I was in the Army, and of course I was but then
a wounded eardrum wasn't much in the scheme.

# At Ease

Once my husband's father, army-new,
marched his son behind the family lawnmower
to shouts recalled from weeks of dusty training.
Khaki crackled under tightened belt as Dad,
crew cut graying only slightly then, bristled
through those years. Too old for overseas
he manned a home battalion instead
of foxhole, but felt he did it right. When war

was done and kids weren't what
they used to be, he'd slam the door
and take a walk. He didn't know what else
to yell, the way they shouted back.
His two girls snickered as his only boy,
grown tall and surly, had to bend for Dad
to check his cut of hair. Red-faced,
sweating across furred upper lip, the boy
finally wouldn't stoop. His father nearly
hit him, then shook as though an army'd gone
berserk, or worlds of grass had turned
against him in one rampant weed.

Now they're two gray men, one
older, but both well pleased with
what they see: a little of themselves.
Hands in loosened pockets, they smoke
their pipes and lean against the mantel,
pace their talk of weather with ceremony
as if slow marching to muted drums. Even
though they listen to each other's voices, loud
but not commanding, they seem to hear instead
some faint, familiar music from high ground.

I watch the two together from another room,
becoming a judge of men, but moved to offer
them a kind of mercy. In two German mugs
left home by our oldest son, I pour
their favorite beer. Those two fathers
now have time to stand at ease, freed
from what they thought they had to do.
They drink, look into their own smoke,
fiddle with keys, and wander into fields
of mist and silence.

# Fungus Considered

I tell my closest friend, Carolyn, on the phone,
who's smoking all natural cigarettes in Philadelphia,
that Blackspot is taking over the rose garden.
I shudder at the inheritance that came with this
hundred-year-old house Jeremy and I bought
from a dead Chemist, who lovingly planted each spiny
shrub with bare hands. *Downy Mildew massacred*
*grape vines in France, 1885, killed off so many*
*vineyards that the rootstock was lost—the French had to*
*import American grapes, which carried with them*
*a new fungus.* Think of it, she exclaims, *imagine*
*the empty cellars of the French, who for years*
*couldn't drink new wine.* A century later, Carolyn
studies life cycles of fungi from a book called *Plant Disease:*
*Biology and Social Impact* where her nightmares
breed into spongy growths. She tells me how
in Ceylon, now Sri Lanka, the coffee plantations were
devastated; the potato famine in Ireland begun from a single
spore, which she reminds me, can and do exist
everywhere. I remember clearly
the tiny run-down house where we lived
together—and the mushrooms that crept
through a crack in the foundation

to settle beside the toilet in the middle of the night
while we rotted ourselves with gin.
*But Bob's roses,* I whisper, trying
to stop the germination of rust
and powdery mildew, of smuts and ergots.
This Chemist, who died just steps from
his now infected Floribundas, his Miniatures, and
his Hybrid Teas, must have hand picked

each plant for its name softly
sliding from his tongue. I tell Carolyn
their names to escape this talk of disease.
I say: *Ballerina, Little Darlin',*
*Mermaid.*

Carolyn's dad builds
furniture in his workshop after the whistle
blows him home. Chiseling away
each night until retirement, whittling
years, he fantasizes
sculpting narrow boxes of maple
or staircases of pine that wind their way
to the landing where his wife might sit
rocking in an oak chair he molded
to her curves, gently, by hand.
Jeremy's old man falls
asleep during every movie aired
since '65. Head bobbing, breath
shallow, he's an industrial designer who

creates the outsides of things that only
have insides. Before the credits
of Zhivago rolled, he had dreamt
of a telephone, so small, it would fit
clam-like in his palm. For some thirty years
he shyly slipped the collapsing
invention in his shirt pocket, waiting
for his turn—waiting for a flick
that might keep him awake.
My own deaf archivist of a father
never built a damn thing. Buried
nearly two decades in a box not made
by Carolyn's father, having never nodded off
in a velvet-seated theatre, because he would've only
heard vibrations, my father just saved

coffee mugs, priceless coins we sold to pay
hospital bills—anything handwritten, stolen: nondescript
ashtrays from diners across Illinois and card catalogue
entries of missing books from the library
he never went to. At the end my father left no residue.
But the Chemist? Had he gone to prune
the tiny buds? To protect each flower
from the infestation of disease that had begun
to take root in his mind, or to shield them
from the coming winter? I can never
not see his body, splayed
at the bottom of the porch steps where I now scoop
deadwood from climbing roses, thicker than
bone, into a thirty-pound waste bag, where
for the second time in my life, at the bottom
of a staircase, I collect the rotting pile

of a man's years. *Trumpeter, Country Dancer,
Apothecary.* In this garden,

planted by a man who knew everything
was capable of destroying itself
stands the daughter of another
whose dowry is the knowledge of how
easily we mold inward. Like this poem,
fungus begins as an abnormal growth
in a wound that should have already healed.
And if I knew how, I might raise my voice
so loud that even he could hear: *Fair Bianca,
Flutterbye, Matador, Altissimo, Eden.*

# When My Dead Father Called

Last night I dreamt my father called to us.
He was stuck somewhere. It took us
A long time to dress, I don't know why.
The night was snowy; there were long black roads.

Finally, we reached the little town, Bellingham.
There he stood, by a streetlamp in cold wind,
Snow blowing along the sidewalk. I noticed
The uneven sort of shoes that men wore

In the early Forties. And overalls. He was smoking.
Why did it take us so long to get going? Perhaps
He left us somewhere once, or did I simply
Forget he was alone in winter in some town?

# Elvis Decides to Become a Monk

Because he has been reading *Autobiography of a Yogi*,
*The Leaves of Maya's Garden*, and Krishnamurti's *The First and Last
Freedom*.
Because he has been meditating and has stopped having sex,
and because he has prayed for months
for a clear sign which finally in the desert on the way to L.A.
revealed itself as Joseph Stalin in the clouds,
which was about his more evil self,
so he surrendered himself completely among the Joshua trees
and his heart was pierced, and when it exploded
he saw the face of Christ and the truth of existence.

Because this life of hotel rooms and limousines
is already a monastery,
every human contact a mirror in the face.
Because Dolores Hart became a nun.
Because the Assembly of God preacher taught him better than this life —
not this Elvis Presley but the plain boy
God shaped out of the earth like a saguaro cactus.
Because he has pressed his precious guitar-playing hands
against the cactus spines to ground at last the pain
that has been flying through the air
like lightning bolts.

# Catechism of the Sea

With a premonition of light the sea sang. —Octavio Paz


In those days, we accepted the spindrift
       from the breakers, the glitter

On the high wings of birds as the bright
       evidence of a life everlasting.

Corroboration arrived in the alliteration
       of waves, a tender star or two

Clinging to the tassel ends of heaven,
       a cloud, light as our paper souls,

cleaned and pressed like a Sunday suit. We were
       given to the immaculate sands,

The incomparable charity of the sky,
       and in autumn, only minor

Disruptions of dust spun up at street corners,
       the glint from mica and the foil

Of gum wrappers causing us to momentarily
       close our eyes—as close as we came

To death, unrecognized there or in the storm
       troughs spiking a slate-dark sea.

Our hearts were white as our uniform shirts,
       as the wild fields of alyssum,

And I learned nothing of set theory and equations
      scrawled across the blackboards,

Was sent out to clap erasers, returning with the unequal
      properties of silence and covered

In a powdered veil of chalk, happily, for years, taken
      as I was with the wobbly grandeur

Of the blue. Now, so much lost, so much taken away
      with the absolute gravity, grind,

Spin and brine of every invisible law, phrases
      fly out the window to no one,

More darkness recited among the stars.
      Whatever I've been talking about

No longer seems to be the point—the ocean,
      can't breathe, the revisions

Of the past will never save us now. It's all
      a fog inside me, refusing to burn off,

To offer up the rote responses to the choruses
      of salt testifying to nothing,

The nonsense it all comes to like the first
      day of summer and school reports

For science torn from my binder and tossed
      onto the winds, so help me.

Now alone, I see the clouds under sail,
      embarking out there for a port

Where the air ends, where all that waits
        for us is the heavy ringing of

The sea's dull bells. Pick any five men
        mumbling in their coats, drifting

On the cliff-side benches, an onshore breeze
        at their unmetaphysical throats,

And see how many words of allegiance or joy
        can be squeezed out at this late date.

Make something of the one palm tree whose green
        fronds are comparatively glorious

And resist the graceless rip and undertow—
        it's just that way with God.

# What a Boy Does Not Say

Of course I gave in.
          I was fifteen
and his tongue was on the nape
          of my neck,
the small of my back,
          its many flames
all with one purpose,
          Then he was pressing
against me. He was fire
          that could pass through
any closed door,
          a man so powerful
I almost believed
          I'd been entered
by light itself, a prince
          who'd undressed me
as if I were the only
          country he wished to rule.
How could I button the shirt
          I'd worn yesterday,
zip up the pants
          my mother had bought me,
tie my shoes, grab my homework,
          catch the bus,
later, at football practice,
          endure the ordinary
crashing of one body against
          another, the common

nakedness of boys
            in the shower,
the little blood washing off,
            missed blocks,
interceptions, a day's
            minor conquests?

# Noodling

If there wasn't a full moon over Naples when
Acini de Pepe felt so lonely he thought he would die,
then there should have been. So it wasn't
very strangolopreti that he decided to leave
his mazzani & pappardelle to find himself
a beautiful wife. He put his best pair
of panciuti in a sack and hopped into a ravioli,
not knowing where he was going, but just
that he'd have to sail farfalle away.
It was hot. There was no wind. He wiped
his mastaccioli with his sleeve, put his elbow
to the orzo and began to rotelli. Hungry
and tired when he arrived the next morning
at Capri, Acini de Pepe knew that a beautiful wife
from that island would be a real trofie. There was just one
hitch. Girls from Capri were known to think of boys
from Naples as vermicelli. So he changed
into his best manicotti and paced back and forth
and up and down the docks. Soon he met a girl
with a pair of gramigna gigante, and asked her
if she'd like to walk a little. *Up your anellini, Bud,*
was her sedani ritorti. Creste-fallen, Acini de Pepe
didn't give up, but told the next pretty gemelli that he
was a rich Bolognese looking for a delizie girl to share
his lasagna. Her eyes scoured his duds, poor
by Capri standards, and she knew he was fibbing. *I'm not*
*one of those girls you can perciatelli*
*with a few dolari, or stringozzi with the promise*
*of bigoli riccini,* she said in a huff. The next beauty
said that he was probably one of those boys who
would tagliatelle out of school. And another, noticing the ziti
covering his upper lip, said she wasn't interested

in a pizzoccheri. Acini de Pepe was beginning to realize
what sheer tortellini it would be to find a truly
gorgeous wife. Lonelier than ever, his little pennine
aching, he decided to wed the very next woman
he met. He walked to the town square and spotted
one buying funghini at a stall. Wearing a tight
corzetti, her fazzoletti still spilled extra
virgin olive oil out and over it, and she
smelled ofelle, like the docks. Tubetti,
thought Acini de Pepe, remembering the promise he'd made
to himself. When he asked, *will you marubini me?* she jumped
at the chance. Acini de Pepe and his bigoli
trofie never returned to Naples. He became
a bucatini and, to this day, by sun and stellini, plies
the malloreddus seas in his gnocchetti regati
with his many children and wife who spoon feeds him
pasta shaped like small hats the size of a nickel.

# Hawthorne Metal, Detroit, 1939

Michelangelo didn't lose any fingers
midnights there, like so many men on hubcap assembly,
jamming sheet metal into punch
press. In the same motion, beating hissing
jaws by seconds and lifting it out,
where any slip of muscle or concentration
would chop down to the knuckle.
With pulse of small wheels, clank
of wrenches, you could hear him set the broken
jobs, curse beautifully in Italian.

Sundays he'd sleep late under Muscatel
unless the machines at Hawthorne conked,
so bad once the foreman Red, who called
him *wop*, came to dinner. I had to
haul the coal, roll the potato
dumplings and replace the melamine
with Andalucian china
before Mama raised the ancient
*pizzale* with boiling
gnocci and angel hair.

Over the rim of a wine glass
Red breathed in the thin sage
of the Carbonieri, and before our seeing-eye Zenith
blubbered at the fate of Don Giovanni,
or lit the ten-cent cigars of a host whose name
ended in a soft vowel, who boasted
the moon was Rome, the sun Detroit.
Into whose grip Red fumbled his limp curled hand
that day, calling him Mr.
Cafagña, Mr. Michael *Angelo* Cafagña.

# My Required Tool

Every street kid in Bombay knows
how to make Karma, but I'm sweating
under her weight like Bukowski
the night he balled that 300 pound
daughter of joy in Philadelphia.
Exposing her eight fold path to find
enlightenment mashed in a mantra
of popped springs. Reduce gravity's
inverse square law down to one
easy step and ignite a bonfire
of spiritual bliss, but failing
this, apply Ockham's razor to
the wrists. These ashes meet Jerry
G's mingling in a whirling dervish
down the Ganges. Won't it be cool
when the bathing medjoub soaks us
both through his blotter skin?
But maybe that glorious pyre will
lead us back to scanning American
burbs for signs of extraordinary
life. At Friday night's party
my rejected friend cried, the moon
will take me long before you
or Raymond. I turned from her
silent and aloof. Wishing we
could forget this cosmic crap
regarding love and luck's
birth. But it's impossible when
we're left naked on the Himalayan
ledge of our final night, bowled
over by a paradoxical vision.
Those who escaped universal laws

never strip-searched this. They hid
the Tao of Pooh in their pants to
smirk and wink like Buddha did. So,
I'll never side-step Karma's huge
body slam keeping me pinned a few
lives longer. No matter how swift I
feel racing through back-ass districts
in a Jinrikisha, looking for a bevy
of skinny girls to screw.

# Going Wrong in the House of Neptune

The billowing cloth napkin still tucked into my collar
surely gave me away. I was a six-year-old in a hurry,
sailing into the wrong restroom in the middle of my family's
semiannual-flirtation-with-elegance Sunday dinner
at The House of Neptune Restaurant. I had to go bad, so
it barely occurred to me: this room full of women lining up
for their mysterious ablutions. They didn't seem real
horrified to find me, out of nowhere, among them — not even
a little annoyed. They continued talking softly, beautiful
in another language, laughing as if they couldn't possibly be
holding anything in. And my small urgency paled.

They were everywhere. On cushioned seats in front of mirrors.
Bowing over sinks where the fixtures gleamed like jewels
in some fantastic, untold realm. Those perfumes, lotions, and powders
knocked the young wind clean out of me: one more explorer
looking for a shorter route to the spices, blown off course,
stumbling into a New World he never bargained for,
so unfathomably exotic there's no going home even accidentally
to the man he was — if there's any going home at all.
                                    I would know
soon enough: on my time-honored side of the bathroom story,
nothing's worth that kind of waiting for. I'd find myself
standing on the other side of that wall, trying hard
to take my rightful place in a row of men gazing straight ahead,
getting nowhere. We're clearing our throats, spitting if we have to,
listening for the slightest trickle of inspiration. If none comes
we hit the flusher anyway for show, careful not to say
a word, and walk away solemn, too full of ourselves.
An Ace comb once through the hair, and we're gone.

I needed those ladies-in-waiting to realize I'd made
an honest mistake. So there I was, owning up to a few puny things
I could be sure of: my name, my precarious and forgivable age,
everything I'd already had to eat, how many Cokes I'd downed
so far. For a moment it was the easiest I'd ever be among women.
When one of them winked and said, *Sweetheart, why not*
*ask for a cherry in your soda next time*, I was painfully
aware of my ticklish position: old enough to be fascinated, but
too young for any lasting excitation. I wanted to crack wise,
or I wanted to kiss her and run. I wanted to piss
with the big dogs, whatever that exactly meant
I'd gone and done. I caught a glimpse of the future,
for what it was worth, the white slip showing underneath
her flowery dress. It was summer and salt air,
and The House of Neptune would never seem so enormous again.

I wanted to be remembered, to go down in history for being
the first to discover Something Big: a continent, an ocean
that changed the shape of the world forever. But I wasn't Columbus,
Balboa, or Vasco da Gama. I was just a kid in a seersucker suit
a long way from home, my whole life ahead of me
the only uncharted water I'd be crazy enough to wade through.
And maybe it was thinking of that, or the Cokes, or the waves
pounding the Jersey shore not far from the table window
where my parents were beginning to wonder, but suddenly
what I felt was uncontainable. And I couldn't wait. I really
really really had to go.

# Going Out for Cigarettes

It's a story as famous as the three little pigs:
one evening a man says he is going out for cigarettes,
closes the door behind him and is never heard from again,
not one phone call, not even a postcard from Rio.

For all anyone knows, he walks straight into the distance
like a line from Euclid's notebooks and vanishes
with the smoke he blows into the soft humid air,
smoke that forms a screen, smoke to calm the bees within.

He has his fresh pack, and overcoat with big pockets.
What else does he need as he walks beyond city limits,
past the hedges, porch lights and empty cars of the suburbs
and into a realm no larger than his own hat size?

Alone, he is a solo for piano that never comes to an end,
a small plane that keeps flying away from the earth.
He is the last line in a poem that continues off the page
and down to a river to drag there in the cool flow,

questioning the still pools with its silver hook.
Let us say this is the place where the man who goes out
for cigarettes finally comes to rest: on a riverbank
above the long, inquisitive wriggling of that line,

sitting content in the quiet picnic of consciousness,
nothing on his mind as he lights up another one,
nothing but the arc of the stone bridge he notices
downstream, and its upturned reflection in the water.

# The Violence

We must try to rid evil of our character, the president says.

The president is paling, another mouth of extinction, suggested the Fox.

I said over here, goddam it, and not in the garage. I was
fourteen,

and learning to drive,
I knew the beloved must not be a monster in the head.

And so, the world sins, it is exhausted, ministering to the misbegotten.

And so, shuttered in the subway, a murderer
rides between cars, so that he is before the wrong,
and the dead wrong, brother.

I was far from home. He held up a blank sign and I let him in the car. I did not want to
tarry.

My beloved is not
a monster in the head, my beloved is either
God's vengeance or his love,

entrails or insight,
I can only give you my word, though the fire in my eyes
is almost
his fire.

Genet:   "A miracle is unclean: the peace I was searching for
in the latrines and that I'm seeking
in remembrance is a reassuring and silky peace."

Heraclitus:        "Come in, there are Gods here, too.
                  Don't be a stranger at the threshold."

In the tear of the pattern
no fleece shall cover you,
no seed-time, no unguent, no mystical birds, no eternal variant, gentian, algebraic,

no
eloquent
        alcohol, in the tear of the pattern,
no weed-grown

trail where a person could rest
in one
of a few mutilated copies—

Our no God sitting low on the other half of the tree, her shroud drawn over her hair—

Then take the cloth up again, the president says.

In the tear of the pattern, the wolf is whole, suggested the Fox.

And you are most vile.
You are a threshold spikily
gone through.

So this is your winter body, so this is your summer ass.

Sunlight glints over the breasts and the early evening newspaper, God's vengeance,
or his love,

whose voice
so lightly      come of wounds

who loves      this way—

# Fathers and Sons

When the day comes my son looks through me
I will be ready as my father was not,
a father who took refuge that day in totem silence.
But now my son is too tiny even for the blind worship
I saw spark the eyes of a four-year-old
across the aisle last Sunday morning on the bus.
And the father, twenty maybe, skin blotched from the flask
he drew from his jeans each time we braked from a town,
swatted, as if he could bat away some ache,
every time the little one lay a hand across his chest.
Neither had stopped trading love when I got off.

I dream my son will arrive at epiphany, manly, violent.
It will strip him like a young brave
walking naked into the brush when his body
stops at its full height. It will last one night
and finish at dawn when he refuses to come home but must—
his own camp set up, the ground burned and staked,
the crossed sticks erected, the skins stretched to fit
that ancestral concept, a tepee of his own.
He'll be dressed unlike me in some hide he has tanned,
and about ready to parlay, whooping in place,
he'll call the powwow, meet me on the line,
attempt half the talking, midway between our camps,
dancing mad I'm his size, red-faced he wants me gone.
And then, on the verge of tears, he'll take one step back,
a signal my father's ghost stands between us on this earth.
This will be the moment I tell him he can wait—
he has time, no one is standing in judgment, no one will—
to take back the blow he would like to strike
if I spoke. I won't speak. I'll be my father standing firm,
refusing a son the blood of his own father.

# The Moles

In this incremental darkening,
short, almost ratcheted turns of it,
his white trousers move over the lawn
as if of their own power. Summer,

years back: my father is tamping down
molehills, dowsing along tunnels
raised like skin above tendons, moving out
onto the highwire of decorum,

like a drunk performing for highway police,
his tasseled loafers indistinguishable from grass,
the cigarette and paper he'd gone to get
become his balance bar.

But he was a king to me. For him,
power lines drew taut, like violin strings
glinting across the hollow valley and our lawn,
newly patched, where the well had been drilled.

He was a king and 34, with half his school loans paid,
digging a hinged divot with his heel, calling me out
to help him bury a penny, proclaiming, one day
my boy would find it and become suddenly wealthy.

And what, exactly, did the moles make
of all this? That gift,
which has become the memory itself,
is a tunnel I nose through.

Our patio lit like a runway.
Insects of all kinds sparking
from the sides of that house.
Through his thin blue shirt, I could see

the dark of his body,
like a shadow on the moon,
like my mother watching from the kitchen,
her concern cast on the blinds,

and then the world was dark
and we were not going in.

# No Guarantee

*We're living different lives,* she says, as she unbuttons
one and then another button on her blouse. The sky
achieves an acrobatic gloom, drizzling streets
outside grow shiny in the dusky light. Her fingers
travel down the narrow row of bone and silk.

A magazine on the nightstand, open
to a piece about the stars, makes me
wonder what we'll seem to be when visitors
from some dim planet come at last
to warn us of our near oblivion.

She slips the blouse, first
from one shoulder, then the other.
*We're living different lives,*
she says again. A hundred miles up,
our saviors are intrigued —
the roiling mists, the steep desire, the turbulence
that underscores the tranquil surface of our seas.

Streetlights mix like pudding with the fog.
*What happened?* she wants to know, *We used to talk.*
Those guys from space are circling just beyond the ozone,
hoping that the fog will clear, that the white silk blouse will fall,
that for a moment we will lose ourselves.

Soon they'll drop down through the desperate air to tell us
in their alien tongue we've made a mess of things.

And we will understand them, or we won't.

# The Goat

Reaching to help hurt creatures they usually
      react in fear
—what do they know of goodwill?—like
      the day on Coomakista Pass
coming on a goat who somehow trapped its
      head in a wire-box fence.
No matter what angle we patiently approached
      it bucked,
the wire cutting into its neck all the more
      till finally we gave up the ghost
that has returned to haunt me months later, I
      being in the grip of old ways,
old goat ways that I never
      seem to slip free of, helpless
to untangle old goathead himself, desperate
      to hold to that one security.
At least this he knows. At least this
      is certain.

# Parable of a Marriage (Chi Gong)

I have a slight thrumming aura of backache,
so Marie—we've met for a late lunch before a movie,
at a Greek place in the West Village—says

What you need is in the chi gong parlor,
so we take a cab to a vague block between Soho and Chinatown
—Marie has to look to find it—and once she's spotted the place,

just a flight of scarlet stairs leading down from the street,
she leaves us at the door, benevolently, as if to say,
Here, my dears, is the gift I've led you to.

We're ushered into a long room like a nail salon,
that sort of intense brightness,
various citizens, each entirely dressed

but for coat and shoes, prone upon the many massage tables,
as we are, in a moment. Paul is a table away from me.

His masseur is an intense, strapping man;
mine an intense, compact woman.
I am asked what sort of treatment I require,
and soon the woman pushes against
various points along me spine,
which on the whole feels
more marvelous than unpleasant,

knots of tension loosening, and soon I disappear
under the specific presence of touch; no more bright salon
full of sore New Yorkers, no more street noise,

shoppers, no more various and polyphonic expressions
of desire, no desire really, just press and release

here and here and here: attention moving
from one instance

to the next. Is that the cure,
for subjectivity to diminish
to a singular point of attention,
everything but this floated away?

All too soon it's over, and the masseuse says,

Your friend not done, you want do more?
Sure, I say. Feet? she says. Almost before I've nodded we're off,
the pushing now exploring delicate regions

that do not seem to exist until pressed.
Somewhere into this almost pleasurable pummeling
I'm aware that Paul is saying, Ow!

and then I hear his masseur say, Your friend not done,
you want more? And he must think he may as well,
since I am still releasing the contained sounds of one
pushed into new life, until my treatment

comes to an end and the woman says,
Friend not done, we do head?
And then as a stiffness I didn't know

was there makes itself felt, resists, is banished,
I am dimly aware that the masseur
has climbed onto Paul's back, Paul is crying, Oh, ow!

And just as I am vanishing into the heaven
of rubbed temples, where no city exists except the one

in which the skull produces a delicate, golden music,
I am dimly aware of Paul's masseur saying, your friend, not done . . .

In this way we spend a small but substantive fortune,

a sum which would have been even greater had I not cried out,
as my masseuse left me hands & wrists behind and prepared
to commence work elsewhere,

Stop, enough, no! To Paul's huge relief,
since he thought I must want to continue,
and therefore he must continue while I am continuing,

even though he was in pain, strong-armed by his fierce masseur,

and I thought he wanted to go on and therefore
I must endure the bliss that had become an exhaustion,

and we walked out into the street relieved,
late for the movies, Paul limping a little,
my backache gone.

# How to Make Love to a Man

Run your tongue down the two tendons both sides
of his neck. Run your tongue back and forth
along the ridge of the underside.
Run your tongue along the ridges of the head, inside his
fingers, thighs, Adam's apple, Achilles' tendon. Wet
the rigid shaft of his calf, the long hairs sticking up from his toes
and the ones lying down over them like little blankets. Love
his ridges, his frigid Soul. Think
glacially. Constant motion, advancing slowly. Remember
penis envy is what men have of each other. Remember no man
can will an erection. Have him enter you awhile
the knee-chest-position to dissolve the ridges. Remember
he's terrified. Remember it's all he wants. Remember
he seeks confidence you know how to handle
his body, you'll grip him firmly enough. Remember for a man
the importance of technique. Remember like gripping
a tennis racket. Remember he's
emotional. When he comes be careful
not to tighten your grip. Be careful not to forget
the battlefields he comes to you from. Forget them, the lies
he must overcome to come to you. Forget that
to be a "man" is to be unjust. Remember his mother
removed him from their bed, deposited him
on the narrow mattress with bars in the cold cell alone. Make
love to all his ex-loves who live in him as surely as he
makes love to yours though he seeks to banish them.
Though he will say so kindly I wish you were free. He
wishes to be free. Help him with trance, wear
silk, light candles, wear levis and flannel, wear
nothing, don't undress. Remember
just dissolve. Remember no jerky movements. Remember
his greatest fear, he won't be able to please you, he'll lose

it, let you down. Remember your walls
to clasp and unclasp him. (Some will resent this, you will know
who.) Remember every man is different
and when it becomes the dance
with each's spirit, when the river is more swift
than flesh, when you break through to the place remember
expose yourself. Let him see you. When he comes be
careful not to change. Remember the ridges
that you roamed to get here, the fall
either side. Where the road began. Where you are going.
When he begins to ascend toward the body cavity
forming a firm rounded mass when the ocean synchronistically
booms approval his edge of aggression, when you ride
his aggression till you disremember everything remember
this is time this is place this is life this is you. Remember
so great is his love he wants all women.

# Straw Hat

In the city, under the saw-toothed leaves of an oak
overlooking the tracks, he sits out
the last minutes before dawn, lucky
to sleep third shift. Years before
he was anything, he lay on
so many kinds of grass, under stars,
the moon's bald eye opposing.

He used to sleep like a glass of water
held up in the hand of a very young girl.
Then he learned he wasn't perfect, that
no one was perfect. So he made his way
North under the bland roof of a tent
too small for even his lean body.

The mattress ticking he shares in the work barracks
is brown and smells
from the sweat of two other men.
One of them chews snuff:
he's never met either.
To him, work is a narrow grief

and the music afterwards
is like a woman
reaching into his chest
to spread it around. When he sings

he closes his eyes.
He never knows when she'll be coming
but when she leaves,
he always
tips his hat.

# A Genesis Text for Larry Levis,
# Who Died Alone

It will always happen—the death of a friend
That is the beginning of the end of everything
In a large generation of sharing
What was still mistakened
For the nearest middle of all things. So, by extension

I am surely dead, along with David, Phil, Sam,
Marvin, and, surely, we all stand
In a succession of etceteras
That is the sentimental, inexhaustible
Exhaustion of most men. It's like

That rainy night of your twenty-eighth birthday.
A strip-joint stuck in the cornfields
Of Coralville, Iowa.
Big teddybear bikers and pig farmers who were
Not glad to see us: my long hair,
Your azure Hawaiian blouse, and David
              ordering gin—first in blank verse
And then in terza rima with an antique monocle.

The exotic dancer with "helicopter tits," or was
It "tits on stilts," was not coming—a flat on the interstate
From Des Moines; her breasts probably sore,
She sat out the storm in the ditch
Feeding white mice to the boa constrictor
Who shared her billing.

So you jumped up onto the jukebox and began
A flamenco dance—all the sharp serifs showing a mast,
An erectness that was a happy middle finger
To all those unhappy gentlemen
Seated there in the dark with us.

I walked over to you, looked up—
Begged you to get down before they all
Just simply kicked the shit out of us. You smiled, sweetly gone.
The song, I think, was called "Pipeline"
And the platform glass of the jukebox cracked.

I said that if you didn't get down
I'd kill you myself. You smiled again
While I aged. I said
The elegy I would write for you would be riddled with clichés!
You giggled.

So now you *are* dead. Surely, Larry, we've always
Thought that the good should die young. And life is a bitch, man.
But where was that woman and her snake when we needed them?

# The Routine Things around the House

When Mother died
I thought: now I'll have a death poem.
That was unforgivable

yet I've since forgiven myself
as sons are able to do
who've been loved by their mothers.

I stared into the coffin
knowing how long she'd live,
how many lifetimes there are

in the sweet revisions of memory.
It's hard to know exactly
how we ease ourselves back from sadness,

but I remembered when I was twelve,
1951, before the world
unbuttoned its blouse.

I had asked my mother (I was trembling)
if I could see her breasts
and she took me into her room

without embarrassment or coyness
and I stared at them,
afraid to ask for more.

Now, years later, someone tells me
Cancers who've never had mother love
are doomed and I, a Cancer,

feel blessed again. What luck
to have had a mother
who showed me her breasts

when girls my age were developing
their separated countries,
what luck

she didn't doom me
with too much or too little.
Had I asked to touch,

perhaps to suck them,
what would she have done?
Mother, dead woman

who I think permits me
to love women easily,
this poem

is dedicated to where
we stopped, to the incompleteness
that was sufficient

and to how you buttoned up,
began doing the routine things
around the house.

# Daredevil

Here's what we've come to see, a boy
in dirty jeans, t-shirt plastered
to his scrawny ribs by a breeze
those sweltering below can't feel.
He's scaling a railroad bridge above
the open sewer that in the hood we call
the Chicago Insanitary Canal,

swinging between girders, the kid
who can't throw or hit a ball
if his life depended on it, a wimp
too chicken to fight back, transformed
before our eyes into an acrobat
without a net, exhilarated
by the prospect of his death.

A misstep from dashing out
his brains, and suddenly self-assured
as that ultimate athlete, a cat,
he balances along a ledge, or shimmies
a high-voltage pole, ignoring signs that
picture skulls and warn both DANGER
and PELIGROSO. He's learned

life on the edge is theater, and mounts
the stage, although he's less a star
than some strange kind of artist, a fool
who nonetheless keeps our necks craned
as he ascends a rusted drainpipe,
and outlined against a sky the blue
of acetylene, leaps between roofs.

Look, four stories high, he dangles
by a wiry arm from Bonnie Caldone's
bedroom sill, beating off while peeping
at her dressing up for Sunday school.
But hey, a dare's not about being brave,
but being crazy, which is as close
as some guys come to being cool.

## Walt, I Salute You!

From the Year Of Our Lord 19**,
from the Continent of the Amnesias,
from the back streets of Pittsburgh
from the little lit window in the attic
of my mind where I sit brooding and smoking
like a hot iron, Walt, I salute you!

Here we are. In Love! In a Poem!
Slouching toward rebirth in our hats and curls!
Walt, I'm just a woman, chaperoned, actual, vague, and hysterical.
Outwardly, my life is one of irreproachable tedium;
inside, like you, I am in my hydroelectric mode.
The infinite and abstract current of my description
launches itself at the weakling grass. Walt, everything I see I am!
Nothing is too small for my interest in it.
I am undone in the multiplication
of my perceptions. Mine is a life alive with the radioactivity
of its former lives.

I am in every dog and hairpin. They are me! I am you!
All is connected in the great seethe of seeing and being,
the great oceans and beaches of speeding and knowing.
I groan and surge, I long for hatches and engine sumps,
for sailors in undershirts. Walt! You have me by the throat!
Everywhere I turn you rise up insurmountable and near.

You have already been every Conestoga headed to California
that broke down in a cul-de-sac of cannibalism in the Rockies.
You have been every sprouting metropolis rerouted
through three generations of industrialists.
You, the sweat of their workers' brows! You, their hatred of poets!

You have been women! Women with white legs, women with black
    mustaches
waitresses with their hands glued to their rags on the counter,
waitresses in Dacron who light up the room with their serious wattage.
Yes! You are magically filling up, like milk in a glass, the white
nylon uniform, the blocky shoes with their slab of rubber sole!
Your hair is a platinum helmet. At your breast, a bouquet of rayon violets.

And you have been places! You have been junkyards with their rusted
    Hoovers
the pistils of wilted umbrellas.
And then, on the horizon (you have been the horizon!)
Walt, you are a whole small town erupting!
You are the drenched windows. The steaming gutters.
The streets black and slick as iron skillets.
The tawdry buildings. The rooms rented.

And now, in total hallucination and inhabitation, tired of being yourself—
Walt, the champ, the chump, the cheeky—you become me!
My every dark and slanderous thought. Walt, I salute you!
And therefore myself! In our enormous hats! In our huge mustaches!
We can't hide! We recognize ourselves!

# Body and Soul

Half-numb, guzzling bourbon and Coke from coffee mugs,
our fathers fall in love with their own stories, nuzzling
the facts but mauling the truth, and my friend's father begins
to lay out with the slow ease of a blues ballad a story
about sandlot baseball in Commerce, Oklahoma decades ago.
These were men's teams, grown men, some in their thirties
and forties who worked together in zinc mines or on oil rigs,
sweat and khaki and long beers after work, steel guitar music
whanging in their ears, little white rent houses to return to
where their wives complained about money and broken Kenmores
and then said the hell with it and sang *Body and Soul*
in the bathtub and later that evening with the kids asleep
lay in bed stroking their husband's wrist tattoo and smoking
Chesterfields from a fresh pack until everything was O.K.
Well, you get the idea. Life goes on, the next day is Sunday,
another ball game, and the other team shows up one man short.

They say, we're one man short, but can we use this boy,
he's only fifteen years old, and at least he'll make a game.
They take a look at the kid, muscular and kind of knowing
the way he holds his glove, with the shoulders loose,
the thick neck, but then with that boy's face under
a clump of angelic blonde hair, and say, oh, hell, sure,
let's play ball. So it all begins, the men loosening up,
joking about the fat catcher's sex life, it's so bad
last night he had to hump his wife, that sort of thing,
pairing off into little games of catch that heat up into
throwing matches, the smack of the fungo bat, lazy jogging
into right field, big smiles and arcs of tobacco juice,
talk among men normally silent, normally brittle and a little
angry with the empty promise of their lives. But they chatter
and say rock and fire, babe, easy out, and go right ahead

and pitch to the boy, but nothing fancy, just hard fastballs
right around the belt, and the kid takes the first two
but on the third pops the bat around so quick and sure
that they pause a moment before turning around to watch
the ball still rising and finally dropping far beyond
the abandoned tractor that marks left field. Holy shit.
They're pretty quiet watching him round the bases,
but then, what the hell, the kid knows how to hit a ball,
so what, let's play some goddamned baseball here.
And so it goes. The next time up, the boy gets a look
at a very nifty low curve, then a slider, and the next one
is the curve again, and he sends it over the Allis Chalmers,
high and big and sweet. The left fielder just stands there, frozen.
As if this isn't enough, the next time up he bats left-handed.
They can't believe it, and the pitcher, a tall, mean-faced
man from Okarche who just doesn't give a shit anyway
because his wife ran off two years ago leaving him with
three little ones and a rusted-out Dodge with a cracked block,
leans in hard, looking at the fat catcher like he was the sonofabitch
who ran off with his wife, leans in and throws something
out of the dark, green hell of forbidden fastballs, something
that comes in at the knees and then leaps viciously towards
the kid's elbow. He swings exactly the way he did right-handed,
and they all turn like a chorus line toward deep right field
where the ball loses itself in sagebrush and the sad burnt
dust of dustbowl Oklahoma. It is something to see.

But why make a long story long: runs pile up on both sides,
the boy comes around five times, and five times the pitcher
is cursing both God and His mother as his chew of tobacco sours
into something resembling horse piss, and a ragged and bruised
Spalding baseball disappears into the far horizon. Goodnight,
Irene. They have lost the game and some painful side bets
and they have been suckered. And it means nothing to them
though it should to you when they are told the boy's name is
Mickey Mantle. And that's the story, and those are the facts.

But the facts are not the truth. I think, though, as I scan
the faces of these old men now lost in the innings of their youth,
I think I know what the truth of this story is, and I imagine
it lying there in the weeds behind that Allis Chalmers
just waiting for the obvious question to be asked: why, oh
why in hell didn't they just throw around the kid, walk him,
after he hit the third homer? Anybody would have,
especially nine men with disappointed wives and dirty socks
and diminishing expectations for whom winning at anything
meant everything. Men who knew how to play the game,
who had talent when the other team had nothing except this ringer
who without a pitch to hit was meaningless, and they could go home
with their little two-dollar side bets and stride into the house
singing *If You've Got the Money, Honey, I've Got the Time*
with a bottle of Southern Comfort under their arms and grab
Dixie or May Ella up and dance across the gray linoleum
as if it were V-Day all over again. But they did not.
And they did not because they were men, and this was a boy.
And they did not because sometimes after making love,
after smoking their Chesterfields in the cool silence and
listening to the big bands on the radio that sounded so glamorous,
so distant, they glanced over at their wives and noticed the lines
growing heavier around the eyes and mouth, felt what their wives
felt: that Les Brown and Glenn Miller and all those dancing couples
and in fact all possibility of human gaiety and light-heartedness
were as far away and unreachable as Times Square or the Avalon
ballroom. They did not because of the gray linoleum lying there
in the half-dark, the free calendar from the local mortuary
that said one day was pretty much like another, the work gloves
looped over the doorknob like dead squirrels. And they did not
because they had gone through a depression and a war that had left
them with the idea that being a man in the eyes of their fathers
and everyone else had cost them just too goddamned much to lay it
at the feet of a fifteen-year-old boy. And so they did not walk him,
and lost, but at least had some ragged remnant of themselves
to take back home. But there is one thing more, though it is not

a fact. When I see my friend's father staring hard into the bottomless
well of home plate as Mantle's fifth homer heads toward Arkansas,
I know that this man with the half-orphaned children and
worthless Dodge has also encountered for his first and possibly
only time the vast gap between talent and genius, has seen
as few have in the harsh light of an Oklahoma Sunday, the blonde
and blue-eyed bringer of truth, who will not easily be forgiven.

# Hating

Tonight's howler blinds
the windows, stuttering our bedroom lights

on and off where your back
barely betrays the play of muscle

and breath as you bend over rows
of ties. But that bastard who

never loved you enough to even
hate you, never

read your words spilling black
blood across a blank

page, news of his death's
a biblical scam where, having sacrificed

his first born, he must've thought
waters would part forever. Now he's

suspended somewhere in the firmament like
the high wire bridge you gunned in that maroon

'63 Impala he gave you instead
of a birthright. Just a boy, you screeched

out of town high on righteous fury but
couldn't stop

scanning your side mirror for the father
who was busy trying to forget

your mother pulling away from the curb,
on business of her own, the only

deal he ever lost. You've smelted
your heartbreak into a life

without regrets, lived
outside even the radar

screen of his contempt, but
late in the cataclysm of near fatal

surgeries and midnight
phone calls, I hid in the hall

eavesdropping while
you stammered on the line, your voice

breaking as I cursed
his impoverished

god. *Good riddance to bad
blood*, I spat into my clenched

fists. So, now you slide
your hands through 40s silks, Italian

geometrics, a garish
print from the kids, and, turning,

hold out a blue
shadow asking, *Is this*

*good?* My heart lurches
like a trapeze artist arching

backward off the wire, the net
disappears at your

gaze, my love — how you ravage
me with his beautiful goddamn eyes.

# Supernal

from "Give: A Sequence Reimagining Daphne & Apollo"


Apollo pulls a cloud back like a foreskin
          on the sky that is his body.
His laserscope will amplify
          the available starlight,
zero in on the nymph
      in her stealth boots
          that leave no helpful scent.
Daphne—who is graphite,
      darkling, carbon as the crow—


                  is out of breath.
If only the stars would tire,
      she might find cover.
If only they would empathize.
      But who will help a person
      on the wrong side of a god?
All largo, she turns to face Apollo.


Though she expected him
          to wear blaze orange, supernal
as the sun, he tracked her down in camo-
      skin, which "disappears in a wide variety of terrains."
He owns every pattern in the catalogue.
      After considering *Hollywood Treestand*
          ("all a nymph sees is limbs")
      and *Universal Bark,*
          ("a look most guys relate to")
      he chose a suit of *Laurel Ghost,*
      printed with a 3-D photo of the forest,
               which "makes you so invisible

only the oaks will know you're there."
Even his arrow's shaft is camo.
        Only his ammo jackets gleam
                        like lipstick tubes.

Is it any wonder, when his wheel-bow
        has been torture-tested
to a million flexes,
                        his capsicum fogger
        fires clouds that can cause blindness,
                his subminiature heat detector
finds the game by the game's own radiation,
                and the tiny boom mike in his ear
lets him hear a nymph's grunt from 200 yards—

any wonder—when the ad said
                        "Put this baby to your eye
and see if she's worth harvesting" and
        "See the hairs on a nymph's ass,
                up close and personal"—
that he turns the housing, gets her
        on the zeroing grid,
and now his snout at her fair loins doth snatch?

Who can she turn to, the monastic, almost
                abstract Daphne?
The stars are tireless. She decides—
        no, winds up—
        pleading, in extremis, with her father:

                        ". . . I am not like
them, indefatigable, but if you are a god you will
not discriminate against me. Yet—if you may fulfill
        none but prayers dressed
        as gifts in return for your gifts—disregard the request."

That's when her father makes her
                    into nature, the famous green novation.
And Daphne—who was hunter and electron—
                        is done with aspiration.
Did you see it coming? You're a better man than she.
                    With no one to turn to—
                            she turns to a tree.

# The Voyeur

. . . and watching her undress across the room,
oblivious of him, watching as her slip
falls soundlessly and disappears in shadow,
and the dim lamplight makes her curving frame
seem momentarily both luminous
and insubstantial — like the shadow of a cloud
drifting across a hillside far away.

Watching her turn away, this slender ghost,
this silhouette of mystery, his wife,
walk naked to her bath, the room around her
so long familiar that it is, like him,
invisible to her, he sees himself
suspended in the branches by the window,
entering this strange bedroom with his eyes.

Seen from the darkness, even the walls glow —
a golden woman lights the amber air.
He looks and aches not only for her touch
but for the secret that her presence brings.
She is the moonlight, sovereign and detached.
He is a shadow flattened on the pavement,
the one whom locks and windows keep away.

But what he watches here is his own life.
He is the missing man, the loyal husband,
sitting in the room he craves to enter,
surrounded by the flesh and furniture of home.
He notices a cat curled on the bed.
He hears a woman singing in the shower.
The branches shake their dry leaves like alarms.

# Torture Boy at the Easter Confest, Repentance Creek

The year Jimmy had four pearls
inserted in the shaft of his cock,
Torture Boy took tusks carved from pau-pau shell
and pierced them through his upper lip,
wore them for five days before
his gums were too eroded, and signed
the Mutation Manifesto anyway. Outer
Change is Inner, would say the goddam
T-shirt. He'd laugh and then begin
to worry that when he laughed he was
ugly.

There was a bluebird one morning,
something he'd never seen, and
it made him gasp. What a girl
I am, he thought, and put beetles
in all the sleeping bags and, in
Jimmy's, itching powder. That
made him laugh

and that made him ugly.
And that made him want to hang himself
and come.
        Instead, he took his knife
down to the creek where he'd think
of the old lady living in a cabin
down the road. She'd always smile
and give a little wave in that old
lady way that pissed him off.

When it got dark, yeah, he'd buzz
past her place on his dirtbike,
then back nice and close and then
around the fucking house. He'd scare her
before he'd use the knife to cut
a lock of hair first
then all her stupid old lady buttons.
Yeah. She'd
cry. He'd want to be merciful,

so he'd explain how the way back
was light already, the water so cold
it stung his face awake. She'd understand
he was just an instrument. He was good.
Felt fresh, fresh as the day he was born.
Yeah. And they'd laugh . . .

# Mountain Lion

for John Peck

He flattens his haunches deep
into the brown leaves —
invisible under the ferns
on the cool forest floor.
It is inescapably clear
he's here — his yellow eye
marks every step I take.
I carried my thirty-eight
for six months after I caught
sight of him crossing the road
until I felt foolish and stopped.
Like the stealthy Bengal tiger,
driven by hunger, not rage,
he's a merciful cat when he kills
with one spring from behind
and one bite to the neck.
Bengali woodcutters wear
a backward facing mask
which baffles the tiger's spring
while the woodcutter walks to safety
praying and trembling — the tiger,
impotent, stalking behind him.

I'm resigned to the reign of the cat.
He allows my trek through these woods
with provisional forbearance
but I shake in his real presence,
wait for him to learn

my desperate masquerade
and walk with a double face,
the one in front that ignores him,
that pokes my way through the trees,
and the one facing back that sees.

# Aztec Father

after an Arshile Gorky painting of the same name


Aztec Father.
Do not call him that because he died

two invasions ago, ordered his own heart cut out
by men who were not his sons.

They brought him the dripping muscle on a gold shield,
set it before the naked whores who adorned his chest

with their fingers, this Aztec fathering a son
who never dreamed of crawling into the gaping hole.

Don't give him a second country when he crosses the border,
his heart pounding in his chest, family resemblances erased

by revolutions he carries in a wood box under his arms,
the inside holding a clay sculpture of his father's head,

the brittle thing rattling inside
as he climbs out of the river half drowned,

his wet hair making him look like his Aztec father,
but don't call him that, or he will open the box

and show you what a man looks like after
a lifetime of embracing his own heart.

# Questmale

In the hotel bar Brank ignores his shrimp rotini.
Somewhere in the city, in the violet darfmex, in the tinkling
brame of flame-slame, Dulang Dulang subtly winks and laughs
one silver second. Brank has a photo of her under another name
from seven years ago. The mopchits keep dremming . . .

Brank sat for an hour ignoring his shrimp rotini.
The panky lights queeped on and off
above the smonknitions. He knew the darfmex was spolfruching.
Wanglangs flackered past in the doilypied twilight.
Seven years ago . . . Her earrings. Her teeth.

Dulang Dulang! She is all shocking hot victory—
she is wink and cleavage and disappearance
and quick laughter in the dark next building,
beyond this flackered queeping, beyond the priz of drem.
Quest is test! Brank checks the mirror. Questiny my destiny.

He lifted his icy Castinella to his lips
and fingered the photo in his vest pocket.
Profoundly pulsed his male sensibility with noir pain.
Wafting through the hotel bar came tinkles of defeat,
endless defeat, panking smubbing defeat perpetual, tinkling

ever through the neo-sleeked naple-tonk priz-slame streets.
But wasn't it better still to be this devoted Brank
with credit card enough for three cold Castinellas
than to become a plump dad stepping over tricycles
and plastic castles in the muffnuff garage?

Brank checks the mirror again, to make sure.

# God's Penis

As usual, I had my zealous eye
on Nancy Morris, the object both of my desire
and my envy: Professor Schneider's pet
in Seminar on Jewish Mysticism,
the one he'd stop his lectures for to offer
some private suggestion about her thesis.
Her seriousness masked her blonde, smooth beauty
in frown lines I'd been trying to read between
all term: was she a Goody Two-Shoes
or the sensualist I sometimes thought I glimpsed,
in the way, for instance, she was sucking
on her pen cap that day? I couldn't take
my eyes away, or keep my errant mind
from unbuttoning her cashmere cardigan.
But she, as always, had her blue-eyed attention,
her whole rapt being, focused on Schneider.
Was she in love with this hunched homunculus
older than his fifty years, almost a mystic himself,
who whispered quotations from Hassidic sages
in a German accent as thick as his gray beard?

During a lull in our discussion of the Kabbala
Schneider mentioned in passing an article
he'd seen in one of the scholarly journals
on God's penis. None of us had ever heard
anything crude pass through his oracular lips,
and before we knew whether to snicker
or take him at his startling word, his chosen pupil
gasped violently and bolted up like someone
suddenly possessed, with a force that sent
her chair clattering backwards. Everyone stared,
but she was speechless, grabbing at her neck.

"Are you choking?" I asked, remembering the pen cap,
and, as if this were a desperate game of charades,
she pointed at me — her first acknowledgment
of my existence. "Heimlich Maneuver!"
someone shouted, and Schneider lurched across the room,
and then he was doing it to her, hugging her from behind,
his hands clasped together under her snug breasts
and his pelvis pressing into her blue-jeaned ass,
closing his eyes and groaning with the exertion.

If it is true what Buber says, that no encounter
lacks a spiritual significance, then what
in God's unutterable name was this one
all about? Their long-awaited intimacy
nightmarishly fulfilled, or some excruciating twist
on "the sacrament of the present moment"? —
a phrase I remembered but couldn't have told you
where in the syllabus of mystic intimations
it came from. I couldn't have told you
anything: there was nothing but their dire embrace
wavering with the luminous surround
of a hallucination — and something inside me
rushing out toward them, silently pleading
"God, don't let her die!" The answer came,
torpedoing through the air and ricocheting
with a smack against the framed void of the blackboard.
Relief and embarrassment flooded the room
like halves of the Red Sea, while the girl who had choked
on God's penis looked around astonished,
as if returning from a world beyond our knowing.

# The Bald Truth

My hair went on a diet of its own accord.
Rogaine is the extent of my vanity.
It didn't work but it was fun
treating my head with fertilizer
as if it were a phrenologist's lawn.
They were on to something in believing
the skull you have is the soul you are,
that the brain is involved in the sport
of tectonics. My skull has a fault line
like California's, which makes sense
given how the hemispheres of my brain
collide: the right side
wants to clean the house while the left
knows dancing is the best part
of who we are. Or vice versa,
I always have to look that up.
They say baldness means energetic things
about parts of me that aren't
falling off. The real compensation's
having no choice meeting the mirror
but to accept that tomorrow
will be different than today.
And greeting my wife,
not wondering, as pretty men must,
if I'm kissed for my soul or face,
to never doubt, as I become invisible,
that I'm seen by love.

# The Utah Jazz

Whoso regardeth dreams is like him that catcheth at a shadow,
and followeth after the wind. —Ecclesiasticus 34:2

In the prison's visitors room, I'm waiting for my
name to be called, here to witness a life left long
ago, a friend I haven't seen in at least ten years:
Jim Winchester. The prison's in Salt Lake, a town
I never visit except to drive through without
stopping, not even for gas, because I was run off

the road there in the middle of the night, coming down off
of six hits of acid, angels rising from guardrails, on my
way back from a month in the desert, from a place without
water or memory. Skidding, I saw the tabernacle along
the highway—without Smith's gold tablets, this town
equals nothing. I could be anywhere dissolving my years.

There are prison forms. Before I'm searched I find five years
worth of hard drugs in my pocket, not counting time off
for good behavior and I hate the beehive decals on this town's
police cars—I know in my heart that they'd love to bust me,
there's no Nobel for a prison visit drug bust, I'd draw a long
stretch with Jim. In a motel nearby is that vacant go-go girl with

the stupid, painted, fuck-me smile on her face who, without
counting, I haven't escaped for the last twenty years.
She's still waiting for me in the room with a fourteen-inch long
AC dildo shaped like a steroid creamsicle, getting off
a real throb on a six-hour boxed-set cumshot retrospective—my
cock plays second fiddle to the VCR. She's gone to town,

ordered endless extravagantly bad motel room service, downed
countless bottles, endless ice buckets, Jack and Cokes bob with
fluorescent maraschino cherries. She's running a tab on my
collection of stolen credit cards, buying wine cuveed years
before I was born—a dozen half-eaten crab Louis spilling off
plastic silver trays set on every unimaginable surface. Carried along

under my arm in the waiting room are several long
boards of carpet samples, *Karastan* wool sisal in desert town
colors to carpet my jailed friend's cell. But I'm way off
kilter—I have no idea why I'm really here, utterly without
a clue. I'm not an interior decorator or wise beyond years
and I've forgotten my real name, need an ID that bears my

soul, something that exists without an alias. Can you hear me Diamond Jim?
I should have left town last year, got off these drugs. In the motel a creamsicle
vibrator hits the wet socket and the pink smile of shaved pussy sings for me.

# A Man Walks through His Life

A man walks through his life
as he did when he was a boy,
taking a pear here, an apple there,
three peaches.

It is easy. They are there, by the roadside.

I want to say to him, stop.
I want to say to him, where is the plum tree you planted?

But how can I say this?
I suck on the pit of my question,
I who also eat daily the labor of others.

# Dickhead

To whomever taught me the word *dickhead*,
I owe a debt of thanks.
It gave me a way of being in the world of men
when I most needed one,

when I was pale and scrawny,
naked, goosefleshed
as a plucked chicken
in a supermarket cooler, a poor

forked thing stranded in the savage
universe of puberty, where wild
jockstraps flew across the steamy

skies of locker rooms,
and everybody fell down laughing
at jokes I didn't understand.

But *dickhead* was a word as dumb
and democratic as a hammer, an object
you could pick up in your hand,
and swing,

saying *dickhead* this and *dickhead* that,
a song that meant the world
was yours enough at least
to bang on like a garbage can,

and knowing it, and having that
beautiful ugliness always
cocked and loaded in my mind,
protected me and calmed me like a psalm.

Now I have myself become
a beautiful ugliness,

and my weakness is a fact
so well established that
it makes me calm,

and I am calm enough
to be grateful for the lives I
never have to live again;

but I remember all the bad old days
back in the world of men,
when everything was serious, mysterious, scary,
hairier and bigger than I was;

I recall when flesh
was what I hated, feared
and was excluded from:

Hardly knowing what I did,
or what would come of it,
I made a word my friend.

# The Men in the Hoboken Bar

don't give you a second
glance as you walk in,
they figure you're one of
them, in hiding,
another bulge in the dim
bas relief of a bar.
But I watch them—how they talk
too loud. How they
shoulder space aside
as if it got in their way.
How they do this to cover up
some faint chagrin,
like men whose weapons
have been taken from them.

And I think how when you're a boy,
when simply to pick up a stick
and whack a tree
you do for its own sake,
you believe the self-pitying way
a father loosens his tie
at the end of the day
or downs like a casual expletive
his slug of whiskey and wipes
his lips on his sleeve
are gestures you practice.
His face never looked this
sad, rumpled
as the heavy suits these men
consent to wear home,
so in need of ironing.
My ambition was to be here, one

of them. I wanted only
to be used. I believed
in the secret company of men.

And now we're all here,
refrigerated far indoors
out of the heat of rush hour.
As I watch them joshing
each other, fooled by their own
suits, the tough on their faces
an expensive cosmetic
already cracking up,
what I see is organized self-pity,
and I'm glad it is dark.
If they suspected, they'd look
at me hard, the way a man's supposed
to look at a girl, at only
the body — to screw it
or beat it up
is all the same to him.
And I wipe my lips on my sleeve,
get up and slip through.

# Keeping

Among the friends my mother found it mete,
In her disparagement, to call "kept men,"
Johnny H—, like certain secrets, was *best kept*,
Till even his unseamed integument
Began to verify the poet's verse:
"We are the eyelids of defeated caves."
The time was past all keeping. Johnny aged
—Enough to get himself what mother called

A "real job" (mother never guessed how much
Work it took to keep a kept man's life unreal);
He got the best, of course: no longer kept
But keeping—keeping watch over the hoard
Of Palazzo Guggenheim, guarded or
Maybe given away by Marini's horse
And rider erect on the Grand Canal.

Peggy meanwhile was elsewhere. Having now
A Fafnir of her own to mind the art
(How much had she ever minded?), she could
Leave town with a clear conscience—to buy more.
Johnny's tale abides, dilemma of
A dedicated chatelain: "My *dear*,
You've no idea what Venetians are,
Even visiting types—the temporary

Venetians: thieving magpies, all of them!
Whatever's not nailed down is . . . Gone,
And whatever *is* gets pried loose—gone too,
God knows where! I can't imagine *selling*
The objects they contrive to steal—maybe
They just keep them: *recordi di Venezia*.

What I do know is that every week,
Especially when the Biennale's on,

The dong of Marini's horse or the dick
Of his happy rider would *disappear,*
Broken off for some vile or virtuous
Trophy—the one, the other, or the pair!—
To deck what mantelpiece I dare not think . . .
I asked the sculptor to *do something* (he's
From Naples, they know about looting there),
And look what he came up with: these!

Which brings to mind my last protector's sleek
Hood-mascot on his Rolls, a crystal *chien*
*Phallique,* conveniently removable
—It was Lalique, after all—when cruising
Rough neighborhoods, as we were wont to do,
Or parking in Parisian *terrains vagues.*
Same principle. Devised, upon request,
For our equestrian *envie de bitte:*

I screw them in to have the Full Effect
(If *she's* in residence, or Alfred Barr
Drops in), unscrew when I'm here alone
—I know the drill, although I'm not so sure
Which is likelier to befit the horse
And which the horseman . . . Peggy always says
'Who would notice?' Well, I would, for one,
But that's the difference between life and art."

# The Mouth of Him

Rule of thumb—whatever came out of that mouth
was not what you wanted
to hear—*Underarm hair! Belly lint! Your mother's*
*a giraffe, your daddy plays*
*string mop in the swamps of Arkansas.* More smarts
in my buttocks,
more truth between my toes, though truth was not a lot
of words came out
of that mouth, even though words damn sure came
to mind if you cast
your eyes in the direction of his face. Thin-lipped,
a crooked slash,
a straight line at an angle, that mouth often as not dangled a cigarette,
or spat a nasty stream of old grasshopper juice, yeah,
that's right, that mouth
wasn't designed to charm you debutante delicates. Man's
blue-jawed & pale-skinned
as a Goodyear white-wall & the jaw itself has a hard
twitch like he's about
to clock you one, but then he turns & presses a thumb
to his nose & snorts out
a snot plug & turns back & maybe even steps up face
to face with you—*Ricochet*
*rugrat & switchback,* he says, *all the way to Toledo,*
*bungholes & rosehips*
like you know what he means, which you do more or less, or
you could translate it
into a story he doesn't tell with that lizard sultry Dick
Tracy Valentino ugly
mouth of his—There was this woman went with him to a bar
& she wasn't troubled

that he wouldn't say anything, or when he did, it wasn't words fit for
    human ears,
she liked it well enough just that way & so she fixes her
eyes on that mouth
of his & when he starts to whisper *Ignominy bowling ball*
*hyena & hippo*—she shushes
the man, puts a finger to his lips, dares touch the holy place. "Shut up!"
rasps she & shocks him out of saying *Bailiwick porcupine rutabaga blue balls*
    as he wants
to mutter; he just up & shuts up & she fixes her eyes again on the mouth
    of him
& her own mouth falls agape & after awhile a shaking
transmogrifies her whole
body & that shocks him, & so he starts up another of his beyond the grave
    utterances—
*Hippodrome onomatopoeia nation states midnight conundrum,*
he says, that mouth
inexpressive as a mudcat on the river bottom but moving
nevertheless—*Fickle*
*altimeter shotgun,* he says, & *wherein are gathered worms*
*worse than facts,*
but now she listens & smiles & stands up & takes the man
in her arms not
for a kiss or what you might call a hug but like you might
apply some kind
of medical apparatus, she pulls him to her—almost *into* her—if you can
    feature
such an embrace, so that he can't get his breath but she's
pig-iron strong
& then she really shivers like she's in the death throes
till she picks him up
& finally casts him aside, flings him like blanket thrown off on a hot night
& he falls on the floor of the barroom & looks up at her—
*What the hell?*
he starts, but she stares him down—*Mushroom beleaguered*

pantaloon! she shouts,
barely moving her steely lips. *Coliseums of beasties &*
*paratrooping oscilloscopes*
*grunge gouge & galumph by the surge of these silly waters.*
*Festoon thyself*
*Festoon thyself!* she advises him & walks out—which was
of course the end
of him as we knew him there along the barren banks of the
Glory River
in those long ago days when we'd fallen silent & paralyzed
under the dictatorship
of his mothering mouth that now says *Pass the salt please*
& *May I be excused?*

# Hot Wind, Provincetown Harbor

Even blowing over the water it burns,
         pinpricks of sand in every gust, hot
                  sting of sun in its touch. The boys are

throwing rocks at the boats — they can't
         reach them; they are throwing fireballs
                  into the sun, heaving great black fistfuls

of the earth's dried magma into the splintering
         light, breaking the water upward. Their voices
                  are like bright arrows launched upward

then quickly falling back. The wind parts
         around them, around whatever is thrown
                  forward, ahead of them into the distance.

Two men on the beach are watching the boys
         from a distance as they approach. Holding hands,
                  the men pause, and turn with a sweet attention,

an admiration which is also a sympathy,
         I think, a memory of childhood, though
                  they see me watching their watching,

and stop, and go on. The boys are loud
         and skinny as train tracks, the ladders
                  of their ribs running upward —

wouldn't anyone find them beautiful,
         with their bird legs and their wild voices
                  the wind takes up, how their skin turns

brown, and they fall back into the water
and then rise up, making waterfalls?
I sit at the edge of the beach, high up

where the grass begins, almost hidden from sight,
a mother alert for rocks and strangers,
for sand in the eye that flies on this hot wind.

My legs are brown and so strong—
I have walked thousands of miles on them already,
as slowly as needed. I am thirty years

ahead of these boys, moving away from them
without their noticing, past the next bend
of the harbor, down to where the two men

have stopped at the edge of the water.
They face into the wind as if against a wall.
The smaller one is dark and frail,

and when he coughs his shoulders shake.
He stands bent over at the waist, head down,
as if sick or despairing. No—he is untying

a little boat; they are climbing into it together,
rowing out against the incoming tide,
into deeper water, clearing shore.

# Sonata of Love's History

for Terri

Before I could arrive at this moment when the earth
wakes inside you, when the night is still tangled in your hair,
before I could see how the moonlight melts
on your breasts as you lay beside me,
before you opened the hands of your soul,
at this moment that is so sudden, so unexpected,
I can only imagine how the softness of your voice must be
enough to stop the insects for miles, and I begin
to understand how the way you open your eyes
to the morning must be enough to change orbits of planets,
so it must have been necessary for me, if I've really arrived
at this moment alive, to have lived
a life where only my shadow planted the garden,
only my shadow walked through the market,
fingered the keys nervously, drove the car too fast,
and it must be the same shadow that curls up
in the corner of the room or is hung in the closet
collecting moths, and it must have taken centuries
of bones turning to light, of rivers changing course,
of battles won or lost, of a farmer planting one crop
or another that failed or not, one atom hitting
another atom by chance, and through all this a single
string of time survived volcanoes, lightning strikes,
car wrecks, floods, invasions to lead to this moment
abandoned randomly to us, this singular moment that is
part of time's litter or maybe its architecture, because now
in this moment which is so wondrous the way
it lies beside you, I either do not exist or the past
has never existed, either my breath is
the breath of stars or I do not breathe as I turn to you,

as you breathe my name, my heart,
as the net of stars dissolves above us, as you wrap
yourself around me like honeysuckle, the moon
turning pale because it is so drained by our love,
so that before this moment, before you lay beneath me,
you must have disguised yourself the way the killdeer
you pointed out diverts intruders to save what it loves,
pretending a broken wing, giving itself over finally
to whatever forces, whatever love, whatever touch,
whatever suffering it needs just to say I am here,
I am always here, stroking the wings of your soul.

# Butterflies under Persimmon

I heard a woman
state once that because
he peered so closely

at a stream of ants
on the damp, naked
limb of a fruit tree,

she fell for her husband.
She wanted to be studied
with that attention,

to fascinate as if
she were another species,
whose willingness to be

looked at lovingly
was her defense, to be
like a phenomenon

among leaves, a body
that would make him leave
his body in the act of loving,

beautifully engrossed.
I can't remember what
she looked like. I never met

the husband. But leaning close
to the newly dropped
persimmon in the wet grass,

and the huddle of four
or five hungry satyrs,
drab at first glance, the dull

brown of age spots, flitting
away in too many
directions, too quickly

to count exactly, small
as they are, in the shade
at the tree's base; leaning

out of the sunlight, as if
I could take part in the feast there,
where, mid-September,

the persimmons drop,
so ripe and taut a touch
can break the skin;

leaning close enough
to trouble the eye-spotted
satyrs, no bigger than

eyelids, and the fritillaries,
their calmer companions,
like floating shreds of fire,

whose feet have organs
of taste that make their tongues
uncoil in reflex with

goodness underfoot,
I thought of that woman's
lover, there on my belly

in sun and shadow,
and wished I could be like that.

# Inside Out

Bursting like an old wineskin
filled with new wine,
a woman exposes her inside
facts, all leaks and projections.

Presocratic Greek philosophers
held that sound
sprinkled its hearers
like the blood of sacrifice.
Excesses of sound—such as
yammer yawl warble wail—a coarse
reckoning
of an evil
disposition. A woman seeding
her sound like pollen
in late spring makes men
uneasy, congested. All

depends on
the pit and loom
the low sapped sway
of the testicles, weighing
down the vocal chords, pulling
them taut and rod-like, quivering
as a tight-stretched tendon
hums. A sturdy
thrilling, not a mere
shivering. Still

every sound's
autobiographical, every withdrawn
syllable is a lie. There
are women and wolves
together, shrieking in the thickets
Oloyga! Eleleu! Alala!
There are women cackling,
roaring like a battle
unbounded by men
in the sagging muscle
of their restraint. It
is the sound of devout
pleasure, the voice of spirited pain.
Call it funeral lament, delirious
exegesis, hullabaloo.

# Nudes

## 1

I was not more than five. A girl in the fields
had shown me what girls have down there,
but only a glimpse before our parents were
around us with their hoes, so for all the years
of childhood and on into adolescence, I had
only that one clue, and nothing to do with it,
but read, pouring myself into the classics,
prying at the boulders of titles that seemed apt—
*The Secret Garden? The Anatomy of Melancholy?*
In the glass office at the back of the stacks,
Mrs. Floyd Baumgardner, our skunk-haired
Daughters of the Confederacy bibliophile,
clipped genitalia all over the renaissance
while I glossed our badly printed local daily.
The buxom starlets in the drive-in ads,
when I looked closely, would turn to dots.

## 2

The power to shock is a quality of modesty.
An ex-Jesuit took me to my first titty bar.
I wanted vision. Also, I wanted to chat.
My name is Fancy, she said, and I am going
to dance for you. Well that is what they do
down here coming to the pink verge without
ever shedding that last ribbon of flimsy silk,
that sequined picket line of smiling evangelists,
which is their only raiment and fashion.
But where did she come from, and how to
this end, a grown woman in a black string,
not bad looking, from what I could see,

with good bones, and the actual breasts.
When I asked her last name, she said, *Strawberries.*

3

Eve, Helen of Troy, Mary, then Fatima:
the oldest man at the bachelor party, I
am not so old that I do not remember.
When she pranced out in the letter sweater,
it was eighth grade again, the day
of the test on South America, the day
of the night of the county basketball finals
when Sally, the sprite a desk ahead of me,
would leap bountifully in her great cheer
and leap also in the fantasy life, making
the names of the rivers all run together.

4

The lapdancer's dress-up nudity is a doll.
Geisha. Self-artifice. Professional candor.
The way the stereotypical male poet's penis
is a feathered quill or mechanical pencil
and he's rewriting Hansel and Gretel.
Also, she's childhood's fate whispering,
"Rodney, don't you remember me?
Michelle. We met at Ron's." I don't.
But blush a blush that evolves from
John Calvin, and watch her squirm.
Part Mata Hari, part alma mater,
her straddling act camouflages
some chatter of her newest daughter.
Her privates against mine like that,
young men watching. Such is fame.

# Doggerel for the Great Czech Phallometer

The phallometer, a device invented and placed in use
before 1989, is still part of the regimen by which
sex offenders, particularly pederasts, are processed
in the Czech legal system. The suspect's penis is
inserted in a box that registers his reaction
to different types of pornography shown to him while
inserted. That the humiliating circumstances of the
testing procedure usually skew results has not
dampened Czech's enthusiasm for the device.
It has been rumored that some phallometers have
been altered to send electric currents into aroused
subjects, thus serving as instruments for behavior
modification.


Beware, you criminals whose vice is sex!
Your wickedness gets measured by the Czechs,
along, incidentally, with that thing
which of your bleakest raptures you've made king.
Divine contraption! Beautiful machine!
No hideous perversions thrive between
your function and the State's unflinching will
to know precisely how a man may thrill
to what no man should set his heart upon,
much less that part of him love's balanced on.
Phallogocentric certitudes dissolve
into their purest forms of sick resolve.
So take the blessed box from door to door!
Make every man get measured thus, and score
perversions on a scale of one to ten,
and only pulse fat currents when
you find a monster posing as a man,

but zap such ones before perversions can
seep out into our schoolyards, all playing space
where innocents their innocence embrace.
So queue up, men, upon your feet of clay,
for even Pavlov's dog will have this day!

# After Barranquillo, before Belize

Near Cartego, up river from Puerto Limon
(With their timid vigils and sacred dialogues,
Or souvenirs: squash, beans, peppers, abstractions),
Some strangers in Costa Rica bleed stigmata,
Possessing the holy obesity of hope. Fantasies
With citrus lenses, sultry ceramic jars
Full up with lethargic rum water
And pale petals on lizards that flourish
With flourishing, all rise like rare maps
From the minds of migrant natives that believe
Life satiates everything in Rita, north of here,
Or, if one is steeled and poised, in headlands
Closer to the sea. Grapefruits the size
Of pink tumors, softballs the circumference
Of disease bring the conscripted, uniformed ill,
Along with disease shaped as other fruit
Or accoutrements of other games. Some
Palsies yellow like pears; some consumption
Feels like resin, helps the lungs grip
Soft wet foppish air. Blackened limbs
And abandoned dark-haired dead
Fill the coast with richness unspoken
In its name. Tired men and women too.
And I have been in Palmar Norte, late!
Or at twenty minutes past noon, or sooner
As a febrile tremor passes along the road.
No, I have been in Palmar Norte on every
Saint's day in ordinary time, and I have
Tasted the skeletons in my coffee. The ambuscades
Falter with gestures of defeat on the grainy surfaces
Of impossible porches, where I sit listening
To the unforgiving bristling of weary farm girls

(The sort sung of by men where the palm grows)
Bickering at the market. The dung smell smoky
In Heredia, at morning vespers, keeps the priests
In a vertiginous stupor. And they, and tourists,
And I dream of the bay Guantanamero as do
The blue men, sincere and brutal, whistling
After the dusty footprints left by a woman
Ambling, ambling to a nearby Cuban farm.

# The Green Room

In Key West, our world spilled gleaming quarters. 1962.
My friend Bart and I would ram the coins
into the stand-up jukebox of the billiard parlor, in series,
paying off bets to each other, choosing that one tune again and again:
*Hey, hey-hey, baby.| I wanna know if you'll be my girl.*
Why did The Green Room, beneath the slow
teak ceiling fans that wheezed and whirled
and barely ruffled the napkins under our Cuba Libres,

while we played our dopey song and our one-pocket pool —
why did it seem an erotic Eden? Foolish, yes, though we were nobody's
    fools.
Or so we had thought, hustling our way southward, bar to bar,
until we hit Hilliard at the Georgia border, where we lost the whole bundle
to a courtly Greek who played us for the chumps we were.
I wince now at our posturing, our swagger,
our rehearsed, fake-Kerouac road life. Two pampered collegians. I shudder.
And yet to have once been so young is forgivable,

I hope, to have once been so stupid. I accused Bart
of staying that way after graduation, working for some bloated reactionary
congressman from Nowhere, Missouri.
I remember charging him on the same count with "having no heart."
I turned out in the end to be right, if not in the way I thought.
We quarreled, we lost touch, and today comes word of his coronary.
No wife or child survives him. So I guess it's *nada*; goose egg; zip; naught.
In that spring in The Green Room, however,

chastened though we'd been by the skillful Mediterranean,
and thus now inclined to play with no one except each other,
the world felt plentiful, the world was all before us.
(He or I may actually—Lord!—have quoted that line from Milton
in *Paradise Lost*). We'd surely find some women. Just now hitting our strides,
we'd surely shortly marry, procreate. And yet we'd still sing above the
   chorus
of humans who merely, drearily lived, and ate, and worked, and died.
We'd go on forever singing to the very world:

    Hey-hey, baby, will you be my girl?

# The Drowning

My mother told me the story, and I believed it:
About the boy who went out too far,
Beyond the voices of older sister and smarter brother,
Exhausted father smoking a cigar and reading the paper,
Distracted mother changing the baby's diaper:
He left them behind and walked into the sea
And vanished in the foam and never came back.
And I promised that I wouldn't do what he did
But I wanted to know more about him, and vowed
To bring him back to life, and my mother laughed.

And I am still that boy standing on the shore
Alone, abandoned by his grown-up brother, or
Stranded with the woman that he married
And their ill-tempered brood, with sand in their hair,
As the waves advance, the spray hits the air
Like snow falling upwards, and nothing will bring him back,
The red-haired boy who commanded the waves,
with a conductor's wand, before he disappeared in the sea,
In the story my mother told so well that even though
She made it up I was sure it had happened to me.

# New Year's Eve, in Hospital

You can hate the sea as it floods
the shingle, draws back, swims up
again; it goes on night and day
all your life, and when your life
is over it's still going. A young priest
sat by my bed and asked did I know
what Cardinal Newman said
about the sea. This merry little chap
with his round pink hands entwined
told me I should change my life.
"I like my life," I said. "Holidays
are stressful in our line of work," he said.
Within the week he was going off
to Carmel to watch the sea come on
and on and on, as Newman wrote.
"I hate the sea," I said, and I did
at that moment, the way the waves
go on and on without a care.
In silence we watched the night
spread from the corners of the room.
"You should change your life,"
he repeated. I asked had he been
reading Rilke. The man in the next bed,
a retired landscaper from Chowchilla,
let out a great groan and rolled over
to face the blank wall. I felt bad
for the little priest: both of us
he called "my sons" were failing
him, slipping gracelessly from our lives
to abandon him to face eternity
as it came on and on and on.

# The Muse Is Gone

The bus comes and I'm ready,
In my blazer and raw silk tie,
My wingtips and Ray Bans. Half awake,
I've shut off the coffee maker,
Slammed the front door,
And watched my breath dissipate in gray puffs
As I walked to the corner.

And now I get on the bus,
Insert myself in the jigsaw puzzle
Of bodies, hold on
As we lurch downtown. A current
Of low gibberish hangs in the air:
Subdued morning chatter.
The bus coughs. The emptiness

Comes on me as I swing my head slightly,
Scan the aisle, the forward-facing
Plastic seats. Everyone goes blank.
The Muse is gone. When I get off
To change buses at the intersection, I see
The daily madmen, evangelists, drunks
Vibrating to pieces, homeless psychotics

And the rest of us — school kids, office workers,
The whole mess of transported humanity —
In a clearer, unwelcome light,
So many twitching microbes
On the microscope slide of the avenue.
My heart sinks. The day takes a nosedive.
This goes on for weeks.

# Post Script

It seemed each morning he would never find the right words for the story. Things happened around him: his children came in with Lego problems, his friends called, his mother grew old, his father up and died on him, his children left the house for hours on end with the car, then came back, years later, with other children, children of their own. And still his wife called to him with chores, chores that seemed only more clutter: bring the garbage to the curb, mow the lawn, oil this door, pack these boxes, sign here on this line and drive the truck four states west, then help me with the corn, keep the silk inside the sink. All this, while still he sat with these words swirling about him in absurd order, words lined up like drunken soldiers, like harlots with painted lips slurring just as drunkenly as those soldiers he'd thought up. But even that idea of words like harlots and soldiers lined up before him began to stink of a lie—how could words line up like drunken soldiers and harlots?—while around him now his mother died and still more children paraded through the house and his own children, the children who had had those Lego problems only this morning, came into the afternoon light of his office where still he tried to work to tell him of mortgages and insurance and tuition, all cares of a world he wanted out of in order to get these words right, get these lost and swirling words in line before him in some sort of order so that they might bow to him, might surrender to him perhaps a moon over a midnight lake, that lake flat and black and clean, the surface so smooth that next there might come a second moon just beneath the first, a moon descending into its own black sky, this lake, the higher its sister moon rose over this lake of words he wanted smoothed for him. That was what he wanted: that moon. Both of them. Maybe even that black sky thrown in for good measure. But nothing came to him. No moons, no midnight lakes. Eventually, too, his wife stopped calling to him, and oiled doors herself, kept the silk inside the sink, kissed the children goodbye, until finally he looked up, saw outside his window a sky gone the perfect black of a midnight sky, a perfect moon rising just like a moon.

One moon, all by itself. No help from him at all.

# Lacrosse

There are the bruises on your arms
    from the other player's slashing stick
and a scrape on your shin from where
    the rock of the ball struck.
There's the moment when you go
    head to head against someone who's
name is a number, in what is
    called a face-off, and you can't even
see his face through the steel guard
    of your helmet. There's that time
when you cradle, carry the ball, Iroquois-
    like, in the basket of your stick, and before
he, that opposing man, and I know it,
    you are by him — oh, in the tongue
of the game — dodging, and running,
    flying toward the goal like the sparrow
hawk who untied himself from the telephone
    wire outside your window, when something
moved in the field grass he could feel,
    he could see to release to, to strike,
(I want to say shoot and score on),
    as he saw a nest, the mesh of a net,
which catches him like a son now.

# Xena, Warrior Princess

Absolutely everyone is wild about
Buffy, the Vampire Slayer, and hey, why not?
Cute as a little blonde button, no
doubt. It's just that I'm
easily excited by chicks in bondage straps and chain mail jerkins,
forgive me, it happens that I dig Xena's thing, I
go ballistic when she and Hercules
hook up, oh man,
it's incredible what that's like. Pure gravy. 100% natural
juice. I'm cranked just thinking about Xena
killing all the extras in a flourish after the third commercial.
Listen, it's not as totally screwed up as it sounds.
My ancient TV gets, like, 60-something channels.
No way is that full spectrum, I mean, it's
opening another can of worms altogether but how can I be
positive there's not some even more red-blooded
queen of ambidextrous rubber swordplay out there, some
righteous cable access babe in skin-tight
skins or tights, or neanderthal whatnot, or silver
teflon space bikini, or that black elastic rattlesnake suit
Uma wore in the *Avengers*, Uma, the uber-
vixen. But what a movie—
woof! Some are born to run and some are born to rerun,
Xena, so let's ride into that sunset together, babe,
you with a posse of buffed-up gal pals, me at my
Zenith of carnage and woo.

# Father of the Bride

It is the cloudy morning
of my daughter's wedding,
and the men have gathered
in the gloom to play:
the groom, his father,
their rambunctious tribe—
footballers all.

We huddle;
the pass I throw
is rooted in an instinct
deeper than muscle or bone,
sinew or synapse, the stutter-
step of memory or the flicker of desire.
At this late hour, it is all I have to offer.

If truth be told,
there never was a plan:
receivers gulped a breath
and scurried; hopes were flung
in fits and starts with such impromptitude
and ardor as to seem outlandish some days,
or inspired, but every generation learns to scramble.

Now the spiral tightens,
climbs its arc and gains the apogee
beyond regret, beyond advice and pride,
beyond long rows, shortcuts, pathways taken or deferred,
beyond my helping hands, however willing or well-meant,
for other hands, outstretched, are waiting, confidently poised . . .
and all is gathered in.

Who gives this child?
Your Honor, Holiness . . . I.
The sidelines blur before my eyes . . .
Attaboy! Have a seat ol' man!
I clap myself upon the back,
I pull the woolen cape about me.
Yes!

# What Surprises Him

Early on a Saturday afternoon, in autumn, a grown man takes off his shirt, his pants, his socks, his shoes. He dives from a limestone cliff, a beautiful headfirst dive with eyes wide-open, reflected sky racing toward his fingers. He hits, a clean entry, and instead of arcing his body, stays straight, like a knife slicing through the clouds. His weight pulls him deep, the quarry water unexpectedly warm.

The man's lungs are filled with air and for the longest time he has no need to breathe. His wife wants children, but he doesn't have the faith now to say he will.

He's falling through the water trying to remember where he lost that faith. Or when he even had it. He stays under, weightless, warm, basic, and tries to imagine just exactly how it was, before birth, when this existence was all he knew. He tries to remember what he was thinking, three decades back, when he was not yet born.

And as he slowly rises. As he floats back to the water's mirrored surface, he remembers something. Small memories from a time before memories are supposedly possible. Thought without language.

He remembers, of course, being very small, very crowded. But the other thing he remembers, what surprises him, is that most of all he was curious. He remembers that he really couldn't wait to see how things turned out.

A moment later, he comes up for air, trying to hold that feeling.

[ MATT MORRIS ]

# Sham Jew

As if part of a shlocky
bar mitzvah shortly after I'd
turned thirteen, Mother told me
we had Jewish blood. I turned
to the ever suffering Jesus's
likeness nailed to our foyer wall.
Hallelujah! I didn't have to go
to Sunday school or so
I wished & blew
a month's allowance
on a 14k Star
of David & strung it
on a short chain around
my short neck. No longer
donning the stripes of my being
another Waspy kid from
the West End, I possessed
ethnicity! Oh I didn't
know the Torah & Talmud
from a tetrahedron, but
proselytizing Pentecostals left
me the hell alone, my shnozzle
buried in shmaltzy Yiddish
phrases as I shlepped along
the sprawling blight of blue
collar houses, frosted windows
filled with cheap flickering art-
ificial trees. When Grandma
arrived, fat arms swollen
with gifts, flushed joy
of the season rushed from her
cheeks the instant she glimpsed

my star pendant twinkling
in the flashing "Noel" strung
across the door. She called
it "jewry" & wondered aloud
if I'd outgrown my present, her
insinuation falling between
extortion & exorcism, but
no squelching pair of corduroys
insidiously hidden by fancy
foil wrapping could win me over
to that petty, three-headed
cloud-dwelling god I'd long ago
relegated to the realm
of science fiction. She feigned
surprise when I took my seat
at the dinner table & bowing her
head, pointedly asked
if I'd mind that she said grace.
*You want to shmooze with your*
*imaginary friend,* I began, her
anti-Semitic slips dangling
like tattered, yellowed lace
below the hem of her brown
polka-dotted circus
tent of a dress, where suppressed
with sexuality under layers
upon layers of old ladies'
unmentionables lay
the saga of her mythopoetic
father, whose name no one
ever spoke, not even the one
he'd chosen to keep secret
that part he himself denied. Still
I knew how he'd died — parked
on the railroad tracks smooching
with his Jewish jezebel, too much

of a shnorrer to drive
to lover's leap when the train
came out of nowhere, whistle
howling. Grandma
swore her father's ghost appeared
confessing he was sorry for
all of it. For being
no good. For believing
everything was a lie. For being
a shlemiel, a shlimazl, & a shmo.

# Once near the Border

for Lan Nguyen and his painting Soul Boat No.2

I was a seven-year-old taken by the current—
On plastic bags blown up and knotted shut,
life rafts wedging up our human endurance;

in the muddy, eddying waters, truculent
with branches, crates, and human cargo,
I saw my father drift from where I floated

and cried to him in terror as a child should
and my father breached the current's pull
and pulled me towards him as fathers should.

Then, safe on shore, we heard it down river.
Each of us stared there, then at each other,
and silence shut us up in its tight quiver,

and in those long long moments of waiting,
a baby, my brother, began to whimper,
and my mother gently, urgently, abating

him with her shushing, with her rocking,
as her hands slipped quiet upon his mouth.
All the while that boat of soldiers came talking

across the wide river and the sunlight gleaming,
their sunglasses peering darkly towards us.
And so we crouched there, all of us dreaming

a dream that would end a few minutes later
with my mother still crouched and aquiver,
gripping that silenced blue body, my brother.

# Training Horses

You are alone with Alone,
and it's his move.
—Robert Penn Warren


Once in a while, if I lie still and am quiet,
I can still feel the trembling, prehistoric,
galactic static between stations
I used to listen to for patterns as a kid.

Marci whispered "Make friends with it,"
and blew into her stallion's nose who closed his eyes,
gathered himself, shivered, and suddenly quieted.

The stable was dark and rich and sweet and moist, and the darkness
seemed to deepen with the breathing of her exquisite horses
as she explained how her best thoroughbred was "broke to death,"
had lost his edge though he still trembled and reared and shied away
and battered his stall and roared and gnawed on wood so addictively
he would no longer stop to eat.

I couldn't read his huge brown eyes
that stretched whatever he saw across them,
but merely by the pressing of my knees or the clicking of my tongue,
I commanded his massive heart
to take the most delicate steps.

Later that night we made love and lost ourselves a bit,
and Marci slept, and I stared into the fire, bemused,
a little buzzed, my divorce about final, and listened hard
to the night that arced like a test pattern
over the little ranch and us,
but could make no sense of the quiet.

I thought it's useless to marry again and again
though nothing I knew could stop me.
Eventually, the thought of him going crazy out there
alone in the dark was enough for her to put him down.

That night I went out back to the pitch-black square
where he had been kept, so I could see his stall for myself.

# The Boy Removes All Traces from His Room

If the stuffed gray cat stares facedown
into a crate forever from now on, the boy will not care.
Bury the cross-stitched alphabet,

the carved Russian wolf, the wooden train,
—where did all that come from anyway?
Even the penciled height marks on the wall

got covered over by fresh paint—why keep them
when he doesn't like the lost kid with long hair anyway,
who cares how tall he wasn't?

The palette shrinks: black, white, gray.
Somewhere he saw an image of a monk's cell,
spartan clean. He will make a box for his shoes.

Wires tangle behind a desk.
Adaptors, surge protectors—defend us all.
At night he hears a weird clacking that might be

an animal in the leaves, and the late train wailing
on its long way west. Why does it make so much noise?
Doesn't it want to go?

# Winter, Voyeurism

1

What we run on our treadmills towards is four TVs,
    channeled today and every day towards judgement.
        Why we have to run
is obesity, back pains, mental ague,

low self-esteem, the usual or unusual daily
    aches and pains.
        Who we are
is running with everyone — running on adrenaline toward

adrenaline — . The walls are mirrors, the mirrors
    reflect us,
        we surround
ourselves, all hopeful bodily subtraction,

all of us running everywhere at once,
    nowhere is arrival,
        all of us unspeakably
watching four TVs convey our ministries, our

trials of taste by millions,
    cuckolds, sad underaged mothers, giddy transsexuals.
        It's Christmas, almost.
Almost it is time

to resume the body's foibles, the paunch,
    the varicose
        insinuations of
the future,

flabby thighs, slack pecs,
    crippling differences.
        Everybody runs towards everybody's story
and smiles or grunts towards a trial that nobody wants—

2

the world outside nobody wants because want kills us—
    twilight crawling slowly with its rutting traffic,
        moon peering
from a tight cloud,

streets the snow has wished into a fairy tale,
    VAC SHACK,
        RAINTREE MUFFLERS,
the VELVET TOUCH the door of which keeps opening

like the eye of some roadkill,
    every revelation
        a veil,
so many sad contraptions, so many blue movies,

chains and dildoes and handcuffs
    without a worldly care,
        the object-silence
of love dolls with those awful open mouths—

3

I click the sound off,
    winter outside keeps secret less and less,
        the streets belong to everybody,
the streets snow wishes into a fairy tale that belongs to everybody.

The Klan now celebrating Christmas on four TVs,
    we run in judgement
        toward four-times-three
wise men with snowy alpine-peaking cowls.

Morning after morning all the way
to Christmas we arrive to laugh and wince at these,
the jolliest
bigot bedecked in sugar-candy Santa beard,

children in his lap, his kind face beaming behind us and before us
everywhere in our mirrors —
I'm ahead of myself —
off his lap go the innocents and one frame later

these girls and boys are dangling Christmas-present apes by nooses
tied to Huck Finn bamboo
fishing poles.
Our assembled jury is all leers, jeering

or are those cheers — I have the sound turned off —
whose mouth
is opening
to say this — just to look is abomination —

4

Inside everyone is a look at the worst,
inside every revelation
is a veil.
Watching the women run, their midriffs sail,
is half the benefit and something
to distract me from this read,
this book by de Sade propped on treadmill's metal pulpit.
It is about
the greatness that exists in the absence of scale
when every instant undresses
to the pure debasing
need to step inside

and buy it all, every published pore.
    For the aristocrats of Bologna, de Sade had two hundred nuns
        fitted with dildoes lined up, erotic rosary
or something out of a Busby Berkely movie

the turn on
    of infinite human connection.
        I also like to walk to poetry . . .
Catullus would like to introduce

his one and only endless theme to you —jealousy,
    Proust said, is space and time relativized in the heart—
        once again hopeful despair
over his good friend, Aurelius

who can't keep his hands off his Juventius,
    as filthy rich as Verona is
        with poor young boys.
He just wants a little purity. In Lesbos, in Caesar,

in the plagiarized Roman columns,
    in the smiling mirror
        that meets him each day—
frown with a frown, and one look swallows him whole—

5

Outside is all look-see, so here again is the parking lot
    and its patron sparrow
        picking at a sodden
bread heel—

because it knows it can't carry the whole thing home
    it cocks its head at me and
        one eye staring at me
like a lapidary through a paste diamond,

it seems to stare through all our jail-cell visions.
    I'm back, I never left—
        human snow outside,
human streets, I drive home past

skaters infesting frozen lakes, woolen ticks gliding
    on human ice, human gravitas
        scratching human circles.
I'm back on the treadmill,

someone I should know is behind and ahead of me running—

6

Here is the story of a king-size bed.
    The unknowable source is lonely for
        paradise,
car lights blow through God's voyeuristic head.

My guess is that anybody's eyes, when things get too hot,
    look away from the subject.
        Discursive
denies the erotic, narrative always ends up in the realm—

*take a look*—
    of the postcoital—
        but when she
touches me I'm home and so is she

and if the body's a prison cell,
    we're clanking gold cups—
        toasting our teeth to glass and ready for this good book
to open,

the silent nights after—
    and so so many.
        God—look down on us—I don't have to tell you—
you are just as lonely as us

for paradise.
    A little warmth, a fire to read by, children or not,
        it is not death or the body
that degrades us,

it is that there have to be so many of us.

7

I leave when my thirty minutes of treadmill are up,
    sparrow is there to see me
        hauling my body towards its secret ends,
my poor mortal god—

my body—
    "young fellow" the old guy at the desk likes to call me.
        There is so little to see
that will not be seen

again and again, and come upon and come upon—
    the old men from the pool who shamble their nakedness
        so carefully across
the cracked yellow tiles and past the scattered, almost

disintegrated bars of soap—past use,
    until their bodies steam like the street grates do.
        It is worth looking—
ice-coated windshields,

trees all snowy—clouds of unknowing—
    headlights shining, some berserk luminescence
        that persists
up and down so many lightsome streets.

And back inside, us, endless, speechless, running,
    dressing, undressing:
        us, steam,
the mirrors even, the pot-bellied mirrors—

it is worth looking—the sights outlive the sorrows.

# Bedecked

Tell me it's wrong the scarlet nails my son sports or the toy store rings he clusters
     four jewels to each finger.

He's bedecked. I see the other mothers looking at the star choker, the rhinestone          strand
he fastens over a sock. Sometimes I help him find sparkle clip-ons when he says sticker earrings
look too fake.

Tell me I should teach him it's wrong to love the glitter that a boy's only a boy who'd
     love a truck with a remote that revs, battery slamming into corners or Hot Wheels loop-
le-looping off tracks into the tub.

Then tell me it's fine—really—maybe even a good thing—a boy who's got some girl
to him, and I'm right for the days he wears a pink shirt on the see-saw in the park.

Tell me what you need to tell me but keep far away from my son who still loves a
     beautiful thing not for what it means—this way or that—but for the way facets set off
prisms and prisms spin up everywhere and from his own jeweled body          he's cast rainbows—
made every shining true color.

Now try to tell me—man or woman—your heart was ever once that brave.

# For Michaela

After this graveyard shift, the escape I want
is not these mostly deserted streets
that fog makes blank as a rain-warped drive-in screen.
So instead I listen to cabbie Frank daMotta as he
drives me home. His story about three blacks
from Hunter's Point who hijacked & robbed him
after pickup, crosstown at a rumpled wedding reception,
each wearing a crushed velvet, baby blue tux.
His head nods, & his teenage daughter's face nods
inside the little schoolroom photo stapled on back
of his Giants baseball cap, until she fills
all four corners of the screen before me.
She too asks for release & asks & asks everyone.
And I mumble *uh-huh, uh-huh,* thinking only of walking
in the dark down the length of our house
to where you're asleep with your own hunger.
All spring there's been only that sweet thought,
and now, we love so irretrievably that it's
like the cab rolling in third down the hill,
and Frank daMotta's daughter with her round blue eyes
and solemn wide mouth staring back, pleading, don't
murder my father or rob his earnings, don't take
anything. Go home. Just go home!

# Parable of the Cheek

Let's just say you slap me. Hard.
I betrayed your little secret,
made a crack about your mom,
slept with your father,
ruined your day.
In the human tradition, even if
your secret had not threatened the state,
or your mother were not a filthy whore,
or if *he* had not come on to *me*,
I'd still desire to slap you back.

Even steven.

If on the other hand, in the Christian tradition
I turn the other cheek and you slap again
to deepen my outrage, I've asked for it.

The whole point is to turn the other cheek
with both immediacy and forgiveness,
an infeasible sum.
Forgiveness is never immediate,
not even for God.

Have you *read* the Bible?

So I'd be doing it sanctimoniously,
which is deserving in the very least
of a third resounding slap.

As for that first one, take my advice
and don't hesitate. I know a man,
brilliant and physically powerful,

who twenty years back resisted punching
a gas station attendant for sneering
at his carburetor ignorance.
Twice a week he still clenches to think of it.
Because he *knew* carburetors, dammit,
and he stood there in his three-piece suit.

Say you're having a problem right now
with this poem. Its banal premise
offends you, its lack of music.
Do you give my book to the mayor
of Illfick, Missouri? or to someone
who collects first editions? to an illiterate?
Do you crack its spine? Rip the page?
Publish an unignorably nasty review?
Write a poem that you think is better?
Do you? Or do you turn the page
and with your wussy little pig eyes read on?

# Cupid

In the polyglot
Unmelted pot of Hartford's South End,
The grocers' shelves sag
With feta and icons, rices and beans,
Irish tea, plum tomatoes, plantains, collard greens,
Something for everyone,
Except maybe the gods,

Who, bored stiff by Olympian views, have arrived
To while away a century or two
In the new world, so-called.
They've got themselves jobs and houses,
They pay taxes and union dues. All but Cupid,

Who lives with Venus
In one of those bungalows on Freeman Street,
Still, forever, mama's boy.

*Get a job, Cupie, she scolds. I'll buy the suit.*

The days come and go, and he's still rolling his rosy
Dollop of flesh out of bed
At noon. A mug of ambrosia-latte in one hand,
He yawns, flips on the PC:

"Junctions of Love," "Macho-Matches," "Heart-throb, Inc.,"
All the dot-coms where the lonely post
Their photos and fetishes.

What's left for a minor deity
Who once brought one and one together
With an arrow's stinging buss? Poor Cupid. He's feeling
Awfully low-tech.

But why re-tool?
He gets a government check
(His disability, "inoperable wings").
And there's always something going on
At the Maple Café,

Kathleen wiping the bar down, Miguel chalking up a cue.
Cupid loves the smell of the place, sweaty, smoky,
Vaguely secretional. His vinyl stool waiting.
Shirley, too, with her chronic sass
And festive cleavage.

*Cupie, baby,* she croons, tilting up
Her bright rouged cheek, swamping him
In flowery perfume.

Psyche, she ain't. But he's tired of that old grief,
And when Shirley invites him
To her small flat on Fairfield Ave.,

When she lies down among her country doodads
And lace-crazed pillows,
Cupid's ready for love
Made in America
Where the coupling's
Diverse as democracy can be.

Look at this pair,
Shirley O'Reilly, Irish-Italian-Puerto Rican,
Cashier at the Worn-a-Bit Shoppe,
And Cupid, Son of Eros, that splurge
That begot a universe.

# Scatological History

It didn't begin in Death Valley
when Dad parked our car-camper combo
farther from the pit stall than Willie Horton
could bat a ball that summer
even though Dad's *Eureka!* woke me that night.
He had taken the pasta strainer
to the campground john each visit since he swore
he'd swallowed his tooth's gold crown. That

outhouse glowed like the North Star
in dusty skies, but not from gold. Bees
buzzed inside. I wanted to unhitch myself from my family
and roll back to our Detroit suburb like toilet paper thrown
when the Tigers won the '68 Series after the summer
I kissed a boy named John who worked
with me in a Cheboygan Pampers factory, his lips
softer than Charmin. So

humor me—it began when, left behind
in a john during a school tornado alert, I opened the door
to a world swirling empty, as if all my friends
were flushed away like the Juju Bees
I had sneaked in to eat but spilled instead. After
that I peed fast in the dark so the kids wouldn't
tease like Dad, *Did you fall in?* The same
question asked by a toy outhouse on my nightstand.
When opened, out pops a man's spring-action cock.

So I'm not surprised I met my husband face to face,
when he was ready to zip up his fly in a baseball game porta-john—
me butting in, opening the door he had left unlocked.
He pissed me off echoing Mom's words, *Can't
you hold your water, woman?* I got hitched
to this guy named Jonathan, anyway. My Jon
calls my snatch a *honey pot*. What a catch.
Surely others have similar histories

or why the word *scatology*? I'd like to meet those
who steer clear of Walmarts, where bulk
toilet paper causes flashbacks, like me, second born,
perhaps also called *Number Two*. And their moms' words—
*You sure know how to pick 'em,* referring to skuzzy johns
dads stopped at for cheap gas, not husbands
like mine who's uncovered life's private mysteries
with me, what those
crazy bees love deep in holes in sandy deserts.

# A Male in the Women's Locker Room

is a shoe in the refrigerator,
a mouse in the oven. Five years old,
already a Y chromosome. No, that's not fair,

I don't know that he's a boy
from the bare chest, short hair—
s/he could be her mother's experiment,

like Hemingway. One doesn't have to be a boy
to shoot lions, shirtless, lean with cool aplomb
against the jeep. But how else could he have learned

to kick the stall door hiding his mother,
to move through space as if he owned it,
his solid body absorbing molecules of oxygen

like m&m's. With his pudgy baby hands,
his skin like talcum, he's too young
for an Adam's apple, though his neck

shows promise. Of what? Not ice dancing.
Maybe it's not that he's male but that he's clothed
in navy trunks and I'm just about

to pull off my things. I could go to a stall,
but he's only five. So I strip.
He doesn't crack a smile—what's it like in those joints

with a cover charge and tips? Now his mother's doing
makeup in the mirror; she doesn't see
the way he's watching me, now stark naked. He peers

across the bench, the scientist dismantling DNA;
I'm a goat in a petting zoo.
He takes in my breasts and pubic hair;

it's all her fault. That's mean, he's only five;
she couldn't park him like a car. But no father
would bring his daughter to look

at naked men. If this were Europe, would I care?
The Pilgrims carried modesty like syphilis;
in Sweden he'd have seen so many naked women,

I doubt he'd stare. At three, he'd be cute,
like an animal. At least he's not ten, or twenty-one.
Then, I let myself think what I would do:

# Interview with a Combat Photographer

With me, the young daughter, Vietnam
was two parts practical joke and a jigger
of censored death. What he'd never tell
kept ice clinking, made him tear
pictures off the wall he tried to climb
in his sleep, or hide
in the hall closet, weeping. In the tapes,
you hear the ice
in Dad's sweating glass
as he lifts it to his lips. Thick
words accent his velvety
bass voice and that laugh — always
waiting somewhere — I don't need
tapes to hear it, even
after twenty years. What I saw
in his eyes: he knew
it wasn't landmines
twice underfoot in rice paddies
or a doomed, hidden liver.
It was remembering
in color — grainy black and whites
the army destroyed —
that would kill him, silent
in the dark of his body.

# My Friend Is Making Himself

My friend wakes up into the
still sleeping body of a man who looks
not unlike himself though nothing feels
familiar, not the arms or legs or hands
which are lifting up to open before his eyes
like two small white umbrellas . . . but it is not raining,
nothing is happening in the window or anywhere
beyond it . . . so it is obvious what he must do
though nothing has been obvious before:
he must make himself up all over again
from the beginning, he must invent someone
who looks like him but is entirely different.
He doesn't remember doing this originally,
or anything like it having been done to him,
but he knows he must leave this picture of himself
in this room with these chairs and walls and windows
and yes, this body, too . . . he must leave everything
he has become and move his legs and keep them moving . . .
so he does just that, he lifts his legs and swings them
over the edge of the bed and then lifts his shoulders,
first the left and then the right and feels himself rising
into the air as if stepping into a cloud and floating
so easily he shakes himself but he isn't dreaming,
he is floating out of himself into what at first seems
a vast blankness but now looks like the street
he played on as a boy . . . yes, he is moving and smiling
at the passing faces along this glistening street
where he began long before he was anyone
he no longer wanted to be . . . just a boy
in a boy's body playing stick ball
with a stick a ball a stoop a world
made out of nothing too . . .

# Jubilee for the Bomb

Blessings on the hunter and the hunted
whose iconography of rifle and bone
whined and hissed and sparked and charred,
on ghostly downtown schoolrooms where
children fractured into half-notes mornings
of Hiroshima, Nagasaki. War
makes so much sense sometimes,
asleep the blood a riotous red, awake
rust beneath the fingernails.
I said something wrong to my mother
who walked through midtown Manhattan
those days in a manless trance. I
said something about Enola Gay's golden
anniversary. I think I said: *Peace.*
I forgot she was there for the paranoia.
I forgot that her man (seventeen)
wrote to her daily and witnessed death up close,
the kind I saw today on the Lincoln Avenue
Bridge multiplied by a thousand, more,
too much sticky red to register, not this
small dry patch that, touched, feels
warm and sad and pointless.
We were eating German food with my
father and my favorite aunt, Claire.
There were all kinds of enemy foods
around us and inside us: things we couldn't say
and things we could: schnitzel and dumpling,
wiener and wurst. Our waitress
lived peaceably down the street, her son
a dentist in Chicago with his own
phobias and retirement plan. Mom plunged
her spoon into liver soup and said:

Do you mean you regret we dropped it?
Who are you, we both thought then, looking
into our bowls for something familiar
from the forties we could swallow.
Here is the meaning of the word Jubilee:
from the Hebrew: a year every fifty
when slaves are emancipated, property
restored, and cultivation of land ceases.
The boy who died in the drive-by was seventeen,
like my father translating Morse code
in the middle of the Pacific Ocean
one year before he married my mother and
they almost conceived me — on their wedding night —
the very first time they made love.

# Douglass, a Last Letter

"Am I always to be a black man, the runaway slave,
living within and without the strictures of a corrupt society?"

In 1830 I might have been twelve and already a rare beast
marked time in my head, one whose incessant growls

meant to drive me mad     unless I could open my skull
and unpen the sleepless thing. Truthfully,

it was as if some creature, cold and hungry, were trapped
in a room with two openings — both too small for escape —

beyond which a sunlit orchard shone warm and redolent
with every kind of fruit, the taste and feel of which

could only be regarded with agonizing wonder and thirst.

Playing with some white children in Baltimore,
it was clear that my life was not to be a life     like theirs,

that decisions had been made about skin and the road
to be taken by anyone born darkly clad.

Being half-white helped little, unless one considers the twist
of the knife in the wound a help. As I approached twenty

I wasn't religious exactly, but I'd come to believe any God
that could author these circumstances     could not merely sit

"on high" while I worked with the lash at my back,
with my head bursting with the wrongs I'd witnessed

and the alternatives to them—which were, in fact, within
human reach. Why do white people persist

in a system that makes them monstrous?
It's like being invited to an endless party,

the central requirement for admittance being
a willingness to torture a select group of others

who find themselves detained as servants. Why?
*Why*, when good conscience must be bled

and good ears made deaf to shrink the heart enough
to enjoy the feast? I imagined God

shared my sympathies, but His procrastination
worried me. Such was the noise in my head

as I climbed the years. That I was not killed by the weight
of these ruminations—or murdered because of them—strikes me

daily as a near miracle. I wanted *freedom*. Even the sound
throbbed like a broken rib inside me.

But I didn't really understand what *being* free
would mean. I must admit that, in this way, freedom

is similar to *love*: none can sing its complex harmonies
without having suffered its long silences.

When I met Ottilie Assing I was already married
to Anna Murray, the woman who made my escape

possible. How could I not think her an angel? How
could I not feel a perennial debt, not matter how

much love I gave? Sometimes I resented her
doting, her kindness      that had a tinge of something

else—as if she were entitled to me,
which, in part, I suppose she was,

though I'd drawn my fill of being *anyone's* property.


Without her help, of couse, I could have been
many more years in bondage. The nauseating horror

of that prospect may never be clear
to someone who has not worn the yoke,

but suppose      today
people began to see you and treat you

like a dog. Though you stood and spoke like a man,
you were given scraps to eat and were obliged to fetch

endlessly—knowing that any discontent could bring
the cutting snap of a cow-skin. Imagine

how long a single day of this would be—
a month      a year. I think you would rather die

than know what I know. When I met Miss Assing,
I had never known such a woman, boasting both

a boiling mind and a beauty that was distracting.
I had not been long from slavery. I did not know my voice

would bring me into such company. The kind clasp of her
bright hand. The way she regarded me unshyly. Her

heavy-blue eyes that said she believed in a country
as yet invisible. Was it possible

to touch this woman     and survive? Even to think it
seemed     insane, but if I was free—

like other men—didn't that mean my heart
should be my compass? Of course, I was married

to a good woman, and Miss Assing bore the color
worthy of my stingiest glance, but being German

and half-Jewish, she knew something
of anguish, too. My heart needed both

to hold her and to lock her out,
lest it appear that I'd forgotten who I was.


Did white men skulking between their big houses
and those clapboard shacks forget who they were—

crying their pleasure in the sad arms of colored women?

I was almost torn in half with wanting her and wanting
to be a husband whose love for his wife could

not be muddied by anything white. I didn't know
freedom     held so many damning choices.

I never believed I wouldn't get it
right—which I don't think I did exactly:

Anna resented me, my duplicity, my looking
down on her small interest in books.

Miss Assing was confused by the ever-changing menu
of my desire for her company — friend? beloved? ally?

White abolitionists, who publicly raged
about slavery, privately thought her sullied

by my black hands and thought me
the lucky nigger with a silver tongue

who didn't respect the decorum
of their generous permissions. Even on the eve

of Emancipation, I knew Lincoln held no fierce love
for those who languished in chains. My resentments

had multiplied so complexly that I don't know why
I didn't end up snarling in some cage, why

madness didn't slake its thirst
on the sweat of my frenzy.

I have worked my mind as hard as any field I plowed in Maryland.
Shouldn't love be *color-blind*? Can I be

much more than a *Negro* racist
if my heart is shut to someone because of the skin

to which they were born? People say wait
until society is ready, but then I must ask why is the world

always ready to harvest the bounty of every
human depravity, while the time for installing

proper sanity is forever just beyond the green hills
strewn with corpses? We make society

by our deeds: we improve our lot by living
improved lives. Society need but shape itself fluidly

in accordance with our best efforts,
right than making its misguided customs

a stone wall against which we are bound to see
our shoulders and the fists of our progeny —

black *and* white — broken and bloodied.


Let us perhaps be overly kind, and let this
strange America be re-cast by too much

good reason. Only this
can build a life that will not oblige our children

to suffer the perpetual extension
of these cruel mistakes. I say this

as a man who, having lived a long time
degraded by men, finds himself intoxicated

still      by what freedom *could* mean.

If, at times, I have seemed lost in my own
unmapped country or acted as one possessed

by a reckless thing, I believe I intended to be helpful,
and truthfully — given what I was given and given

the interplay of passion and predicament —
I don't think I could have done other than I did.

[ JASON SHINDER ]

# Growing Up

The trouble with me
        is I don't know
                if my penis

is too small
        and I don't know
                who to ask.

Sometimes, for days,
        I don't think
                about it

but then I wake,
        T-shirt ripped
                from which it seems

the sea
        has been dripping,
                wool blanket

turned down low
        on the bed
                which has something

to do with dying.
        If only the world
                were blind.

If only
        my fingers
                would fall off.

# Late Psalm

I am hating myself for the last time.
    I'm rolling up angst like a slice of bread,
squishing it into a glob that will rot
      into blue medicine — another joke,
delivered by God, who when you finally
      elbow and nudge to the front of the line,
says, *Oh, but the first shall be last* . . .
    I'm considering the roadside grass,
all dressed up and headed straight for the fire.
    "Who isn't?" say the flames,
though it's easy to pretend not to hear
      in this mountain resort with its windows
all finely dressed for the busiest season
      filled with glass fish, turquoise earrings,
infusers that turn weeds into tea.
    "Who isn't poor already?" sing the stalks
of dried milkweed, though it's hard to
      imagine these shoppers in bright ski jackets
coated with road grit, dust from the chunks
      of bituminous coal left outside mines
for the poor to glean. The poor —
    just driving by those bent figures,
filling their plastic bags, here in the 1990s,
    took my breath, made me stop nodding
*yeah yeah* to the music and pull off the road,
    stunned by the way the years press hard
to fossilize plants, and the poor too,
    who seem to age a month for every
middle-class day. How could they
    possibly hear a blade of grass sigh, "Poor?
There is no such thing." Did I say
    I'm hating myself for the last time?

It's not easy, but I'm loving instead—
  brown teeth, Kool Aid mustaches, swollen
knuckles, nature's answer to all questions—
  prodigality, those countless insects
and missionary weeds spending themselves
  freely and as far as I can tell, never
rescinding a thing. I'm loving a man
  with his pockets full of pen caps, receipts,
crumpled dollars to put in a beggar's
  dented cup, briefcase bulging with papers,
leftover crusts for the ducks,
  and out of his eyes little fish of light,
glimmering minnows and fingerlings
  leaping between us, flashing
like the tiny carp we watched last night
  in the restaurant tank, appearing through
weeds, miniature castles, a bubbly
  tube resuscitating their atmosphere.
Do they ever conceive of worlds outside
  the only one they've known? Because *he* is,
my man says they're serene, swimming in
  a seamless rippling universe,
not quaking at the sight of monstrous eyes
  leering into the tank, not aching
with the lure of light, lethal burn of air,
  declaring their world a glass prison house.
Rich or poor—who decides? Who wrote
  the stories in which women cry out
all the more when folks tell them to hush,
  and beggars asking for money
get wild rapture instead?

# In the Park

Tourniquet tight, spade vein rising, I must have done it
Three or four times before I realized it was me easing the needle
Into my vein. My friends crouched, waiting for their turn,

Our eyes fixed on the plunger slowly pressing down.
It was as close as I'd ever felt to anyone, those moments
We huddled in the bushes: The earth's acid stinks

Rose corrosive in our nostrils, our craving
To see how hard how fast the high would hit
Making us smile into each other's eyes and ask,

*Hey, dude, are you getting killed?*
—And then we'd throw back our heads to laugh and laugh,
Oblivious to the cops or the passersby who glance

Then glance away, swerving to avoid
That glowing knot of energy . . .
Why didn't I OD or end in rags

Or do time like my dealer friends?
By summer's end, stoned on my bench as smashed glass
Gleams at my feet, the way my head lolls back or pitches

Forward to nod and nod, my loosened limbs
That shiver and twitch while my flesh drifts like fog,
Are irrelevancies: All I see are their eyes

Parleying with risk, dense with desire . . . our shared euphoria
As that fuse of warmth in each one's veins
Explodes pleasantly pulsing in the brain,

Lifting and dissolving us, embraced by the drug's
Slow downward drag, our shoulders shrugging in a drowse . . .
How old was I, fifteen, sixteen? Like a ghost

Wrapped in mist, I'd drift home late and wait for the lights
To go out. Then I'd glide past my parents' door,
The furniture swirling round me in the dark,

And lie down in bed in the silence piling
Stone on stone . . . How high that wall had grown
Since I'd turned thirteen: The adult world (and wasn't I

Part of it, swinging a pick for a construction crew?)
Returned my stone-eyed, stone-faced stare:
How different from the park where

We slapped each other's hands and gauged to
The least grain the hit we'd share, blood brothers, soldiers
Of sensation. I'd hear bright whirling voices

Talking me to sleep, the park like an oasis
Glimmering through the dark . . . and then bannering faces
Like opposing flags arguing and arguing till dawn . . .

I'd wake leaden-eyed: Whose voices had I heard?
That wall so high it seemed impossible to scale,
We'd mumble "Good morning," "goodbye . . ." Almost the last time

That I shot up my father caught me tying off
In the bathroom. I was so far gone I hadn't noticed
His routine searching of my clothes, my mother's frown

Egging him on. The shower I left running
Beat down dully as we wrestled for my fix, me groping
At his hand as he flushed it away, his frightened grin

Imploring me to stop. We peered at each other
Through the steam before our gazes numbly dropped,
Mist drifting round us in soft slow-motion:

I'd made myself over, no part of me theirs,
But belonging to Jack, Eddie, Wild Bill—the risks
We incurred now flurrying up inside to scare me:

Trembling like my father, our eyes welling with shock,
I saw myself stripped of my rebel's bravado,
My needle a prop, yet so perilously real

That what happens next seems almost laughable:
"This is hard drugs," shouts my father. "You shouldn't
Steal stuff from my pockets," I shout back.

And then a shame-faced, fidgeting silence
Which he breaks by touching me gently on the shoulder,
Touching me, I realize now, as if I were still

His child, and his touch could fix what is unfixable . . .
Fists clenched, cursing at the waste,
I muscled past him and ran to the park:

Where could I cop, how much "hero" did I need
To buy to sell to make back what I'd lost?
. . . That self I was which only in adventure

Could feel itself tested and so taste joy
(And wasn't it part sexual, that hunger to get high,
Nerve after nerve roused to pleasure?) haunts my eyes

When I see some boy trashed on a bench like mine:
That jargon's edginess, "trashed" "killed" . . .
What happened to Jack, Eddie, Wild Bill? Or the glamour

Of my works tarnishing in the rot of crumbled leaves?
And that boy I was, if I could see him now . . .
—He looks so young, as if he were my son

Sitting in the park, his face floating
In the neon dark as he scratches lazily
With a wobbly forefinger his stubbled cheek

And temple. Now the blood-webbed whites of his eyes
Roll up, his lips sag open, the syllables dragging across
His tongue dragging in my ears: *Dude, want to get killed?*

# Driving Home to See the Folks

Asleep at the wheel nearly
dead I think
and feeling nothing
but the dark eyes of the Wyoming antelope
on my skin — watching me pass — a small animal
growling down the highway with both eyes aglow.

To keep awake
I push my head out the window
as into a guillotine
the black wind and sleet
slipping under each eyelid
like a child's thin silver spoon.

Looking back into the car
through the ice and tears
I do not recognize that body sleeping there.
I no longer know that leg pressed hard
to the gas, that blue coat or wool scarf or
that hand reaching out to the wheel.

Folks, you know I am doing my best —
pushing hard toward you
through this winter sky
but reduced to this —

just this head out a window
streaming through space like a bearded rock,
a hunk of pocked iron with melting eyes.

The trail of fiery mist
growing out from the back of my head
stretches now for miles across the night.

The odds, I know, are a thousand to one
I'll burn up before touching earth

but if somehow I do make it home
smashing across the farmyard
and lighting up the sky

I will throw a red glow across the barn's silver roof
and crash into the rough wood of your back door
smaller than a grain of sand
making its one childlike knock.

The porch light will hesitate
then snap on, as it always does
when a car comes up the lane
late at night.

The two sleepy old faces
will come to the door
in their long soft robes —
will stand there bewildered
rubbing their eyes
looking around and wondering
who it was at their door

no sooner come than gone

a cinder in the eye.

# Terms

This night we're drinking beer a pint
at a time, from Ball jars made in Muncie

where my wife and father were born. We're
doing this for no better reason, I think,

than to drink more and drink faster. Nostalgia
plays no part. The evening is coming on,

the low, wide prairie sky has begun to gray
in the fashion that sunsets take in here

when there's 90% humidity and no wind to urge
it elsewhere. No moon yet either, nothing

but the lazy twinkle of a star here and there
and the flashing red elegance of a light

atop the grain elevator. Somewhere beneath it
Varney sits on a three-legged stool with a flashlight

in his hands and a thermos of spiked coffee.
He's waiting for Linda to arrive, no doubt,

so they can move inside where the scales are read,
inside each other's baggy jeans and body, maybe

inside each other's soul. Each Tuesday before Linda
goes out, she wheels her husband to the bedroom,

turns on the television, and kisses him goodbye.
He's memorized this ceremony of the Purple Heart,

knows it as well as any Veterans Day parade
he's learned to sit through. Outside his window

and ours, too, a diaphanous fog has risen from the beans,
tempting us to name it good or bad, angel or serpent.

Our black dog pauses in mid-field, surveying
the contour and design of the yellow flashes

that might be earth-bound stars, but are really just
fireflies blinking off and on. The males go high

and the females low while they signal their species,
their need, their readiness. All this is true,

but I lied to you earlier. We're drinking
like this because we want a child and we can't

have one. "These things happen," the doctor said,
"These things you have to live with." Most nights

it's easy to feel inadequate, slightly broken,
thinking of the good or even the bad parent

you'll never have the chance to be. Honestly,
we're a little tiresome in our own despair,

which, after all, is not the despair of Varney
when Linda doesn't arrive, or Linda's that she's

not gotten her period, or anything like
that of her husband, who can't lie there

beside her without wanting to touch her
in a way that more than his mind can feel.

# From the Lake

In those days you were still in love
With Dante, & Dante, I think, was almost in love
With you. You'd drive him to your parents' place
Up at the lake, & after you'd fucked him stupid
You'd leave him asleep in your girlhood bed, walk
Downstairs & out onto the veranda, sitting naked
In the moonlight in one of the old Adirondack chairs,
The wildcat from the woods suddenly arriving
To curl on your warm stomach, & you'd pick up
The phone, & call me, leaving me a message, a message
So desperate that every time, as you were speaking, I could
Barely keep myself from lifting the receiver
From its cold cradle, though even if I had I suppose
You'd have simply continued to speak on to no one. That is,
To me alone, always me, alone.

# While Watching *Cops* I Think of You

Cop pulls a car over for tag investigation, something dull,
and before he gets to the car, guy punches, takes off.
Guarantee the cop's *always* pissed. Lots of macho energy
in the cop car as he begins the chase. I watch *Cops*

at 2 p.m. weekdays. It's on two channels at the same time
so I switch back and forth for best action. My ass
on the couch, leg slung over the arm. My guess is you've
never seen the show, one pop culture icon you let pass by.

*I want to fuck*, you say. And I say, *okay, let's*. But the cop
is so mad he calls for backup and pretty soon there's a row
of pulsing red and blue lights. OK, sure, car as cock, I get it,
but it's more fun fooling around with you right here, watch

the chase a little with me. This finally happens: tire explodes,
pops off, rims spark like New Year's Eve or it's *boom* upside down,
into a ditch. And sitting here, you suggest that's orgasm. When
you tell me, I'm already coming, scrape of tires, pick-up flips

three times, car tosses over, rotates on the roof. And every time
I scream, *I'm coming*, though I'm not on either side, depends
which guy's the dumbest, and it's always some lame guy,
glassy eyes, staggering from impact, ejected or head smacked

on the wheel. You know I love danger. Makes me shudder.
Cop always asks: *hey man, why did you run?* And the guy
says: *I have a speeding ticket* or *I forgot my license*, something
purely brainless. And now you love the show so much I let you

handle the remote, switch from one *Cops* to the other.
There's so much tension. From now on, I'll plan you here,
by my side. We can admire amazing conclusions, afterglow,
when the guy's cuffed, shoved into the back of the cop car,
and you know cop says: *man, you're in serious trouble now.*

# Spring Smoke

The minutes ooze into a honeycomb gold.
He reads in a recently discovered notebook

that in 1941 his grandfather refused
to collaborate with the puppet government

and was kidnapped in Shanghai, held
in a smoky loft where he breathed

through a hole in the roof while his captors
unloaded, reloaded revolvers, played

mahjong. He pauses to adjust the light,
wonders if the wasp nest lodged on a beam

in the shed is growing. His grandfather
describes a woman who refused to divulge

where her husband was until they poured
scalding tea down her throat and crushed

her right hand in a vise. He glances up
but cannot discern stars through the skylight.

He senses smoky gold notes rising
out of a horn and knows how easy it is

to scald, blister, burst. This morning
when he drew back a wood slat

to swing the gate, he glimpsed a young
pear tree blossoming in the driveway.

# Table

from the Turkish of Edip Cansever

A man filled with the gladness of living
Put his keys on the table,
Put flowers in a copper bowl there.
He put his eggs and milk on the table.
He put there the light that came in through the window,
Sound of a bicycle, sound of a spinning wheel.
The softness of bread and weather he put there.
On the table the man put
Things that happened in his mind.
What he wanted to do in life,
He put that there.
Those he loved, those he didn't love,
The man put them on the table too.
Three times three make nine:
The man put nine on the table.

He was next to the window next to the sky;
He reached out and placed on the table endlessness.
So many days he had wanted to drink a beer!
He put on the table the pouring of that beer.
He placed there his sleep and his wakefulness;
His hunger and his fullness he placed there.

Now that's what I call a table!
It didn't complain at all about the load.
It wobbled once or twice, then stood firm.
The man kept piling things on.

## Arc Welder

Landfill west of the lake
means the water table
rises fresh in the dig
to rile the guy in a tee shirt
whose Celtic chain, tattooed,
flexes as he sets a retaining wall.
The crane-grapple locks metal
like folds of a lady's fan.
He hooks his waist
to the squirrel cage that hoists him
to the first sheet.
                          Ground level,
grips steady the I beam
as he straddles each slab
chalked with runes: NS 2.11 22'
then clips the harness around legs, chest.
He edges down the row.
His hard hat
molds the shadow of the cable
which swings
over his head.
                          Office windows frame the dark
suits that point
as he nods to the smile
he plays to—the woman
he names *Mimosa*,
whose dress lifts over her knees
like pink blooms from his grandmother's silk tree,
filling the porch glider.
The pile driver covers the hinges.
The girder slips down the slot.
            If the beam jumps its tether—

he knows ironworkers—
he can spot them—
the ones with fingers gone.
She, wide-eyed behind plate glass;
he, planting a wall
between them.
He taps his hat with his screwdriver;
solders blue, then red-orange—
　　　　brighter than the sun
the flame that obeys him.

# Prayer for the Man Who
# Mugged My Father, 72

May there be an afterlife.

May you meet him there, the same age as you.
May the meeting take place in a small, locked room.

May the bushes where you hid be there again, leaves tipped with razor-
    blades and acid.
May the rifle butt you bashed him with be in his hands.
May the glass in his car window, which you smashed as he sat stopped
    at a red light, be embedded in the rifle butt and on the floor to break
    your fall.

May the needles the doctors used to close his eye, stab your pupils
    every time you hit the wall and then the floor, which will be often.
May my father let you cower for a while, whimpering, "Please don't
    shoot me. Please."
May he laugh, unload your gun, toss it away;
Then may he take you with bare hands.

May those hands, which taught his son to throw a curve and drive a nail
    and hold a frog, feel like cannonballs against your jaw.
May his arms, which powered handstands and made their muscles jump
    to please me, wrap your head and grind your face like stone.
May his chest, thick and hairy as a bear's, feel like a bear's snapping
    your bones.
May his feet, which showed me the flutter kick and carried me miles
    through the woods, feel like axes crushing your one claim to man-
    hood as he chops you down.

And when you are down, and he's done with you, which will be soon,
    since, even one-eyed, with brain damage, he's a merciful man,
May the door to the room open and let him stride away to the Valhalla
    he deserves.
May you—bleeding, broken—drag yourself upright.

May you think the worst is over;
You've survived, and may still win.

Then may the door open once more, and let me in.

# Oh, Atonement

Through lonely motel walls
I heard that human ah
of pleasure from a woman
with a man.
I don't remember who I was then,
only that I was
alive again somehow,
so I sat up all that night,
grateful for whatever
noisy business they could give me,
but there was never enough,
so I entered the stream
and moved then
at my ease
with the current
and the dark
shapes of my baggage
through a winding
journey of a life
until some people
murdered the truth.
Yet this evening,
along roads
I have come home to
after the many deaths
and the many betrayals,
I can watch a giant
thunderhead
grow and form itself

like a living thing
into one corner
of our flat Ohio sky
and I can say
this is where I'll pray.

# The Inquisition: A Romance

Am I the same after we married as I was before?

Before, your dainty fingers rubbed my sweet
exhaustion temple to toe with precious oils; after,
you levitate the sheets with exotic winds that pile-drive
my comatose self to the floor where it sleeps curled up
with your ferret and freeze-dried cat.

But am I really the same as I was before?

O before and behind closed doors you'd
toil for hours at your toilette, day
and a night to select a broach
or a handkerchief, while after—my turtle
dove—you lift the toilet tank lid and throw
rusty water on your face, ransack the laundry
hamper and brush your teeth with a cigarette
butt rescued from across the street.

But am I the same woman you courted
off the Northumberland coast combing
the North Sea in a lobster boat where
after pulling a live octopus from a trap
you wrapped it around my thigh in lieu
of an engagement ring?

On our honeymoon when I twisted
my ankle while snorkeling a reef, you performed
a dead man's carry and swam me to shore. At
the feed store this morning you didn't lift
an eyebrow when mister leering Sales

Associate dropped an eighty
pound bag of bat guano on my foot convalescing
from a planter's wart.

But am I truly the same?

You used to dust your flaming
duck a la orange with heavenly
spices, but this plate's layered
with a microwaved glob
of something scavenged
from the compost bucket.

But are *we* the same?

Didn't orgasms dangling from the chandelier spill
onto the lawn under the night sky until
you started feeding the mailman little bits
of ambrosia with your fingertips?

But am I still alluring as when we watched
the moon swimming under ice at Bingham Falls and I
sang you *Ebben?* . . . *N'andro lontana* from *La Wally*?

Husband-beater on roller skates, Bitch
of Buchanwald on rye, when you made me
climb on my knees up the hundred granite steps
of Mt Royal to the Basilica to kiss the hem
of your unwashed dress, I confess I had
my reservations.

But doesn't your whole being
overflow when you see my petticoats
flouncing in your direction? Don't you want
to do that tongue, thumb, and index
finger minuet? You know you can't

resist the lingering
look of love and death in the half-

closed corner of my semi-
averted eye. And doesn't
your unquenchable
yen for the trembling
hills and valleys of my body take
the proverbial cake?

It does, but like crapulent Dr. Jekyl staring
in the glass at Mr. Hyde, I marvelled
on our wedding night as an auxiliary
nipple materialized in the amber light

midway to the other two — and reeling
like a cross between
Beowulf, Virginia, and the big bad
on LSD, I wondered what other
goodies you had in store, but pinky
swear, my nectarous
darling, I loved you then — and now
I dig you even more.

# Sponge Boy

He dreams whole continents of tires aflame, the velvet *yes yes*
of gas fumes when his mother finds him sniffing
the Suburban's tank like it's a dog in heat. Only he can hear

the medicine cabinet, a piñata jangling Vicodin and Restoril,
decibels of cough syrup. Fifteen years old & this need
marrowed in. From choked pipes, the plumber roots out

empty amber bottles. The second sister breaks
down, slips the full tattle, like a hotel bill, under her parents' door.
No use denying the vamperic fog, the eye drops and Tic-Tacs

wrapped in oddly scented sheets. Outside, the family's hedges
grimace in the neighbors' headlights while the sneak
thieves the mesmerized streets. Next morning: everyone's lost

cab fare, and seven decapitated frog heads, like little Stalins,
line the driveways. The devil's commandeered
that boy's gyroscope for sure. If only he weren't

so jacked up, bent, so *chemical*. Box him, send him away
to some brick margin. Couldn't the prospect of a death
tour do anything or the rat-tat-tat of a shrink's excursion

in his sog brain? O limbic skull, his mother prays,
O scatter cast. Strain the savage from his cortex. Let
the twisted thing drip clean from him, feral & steaming,

as from the slit throats of slaughtered calves.

# Chance Encounter with a Wounded Man Playing a Theremin

What he had in his hand seemed to be the handle
to a case one would carry his theremin in
back in the days when theremins were all the rage.
Did we really call him J. R. or was his name altogether
different and J. R. his way of hoping to get us
to take him seriously by being kind of funny?
But he didn't have a thing in his hand.
He moved his hand around an idea the way a man would
move his left hand around a theremin's left antenna
in order to begin to learn how to play it.
His right hand had been bandaged up and hidden
from us for reasons we could never fathom.
And we didn't know him well enough, we thought,
to ask. What if the answer to our question
turned out to be an embarrassment or worse,
shameful or filled with pain?
Still he could use the bandaged hand to manipulate
the airwave around the right antenna of his theremin
which he did whenever he could spare a little time
he would stand with his feet parallel to the legs
of the stand on which he'd set up his theremin
and begin moving his hands and thus begin learning
how to play the theremin.
We watched him in amazement. Our eyes popped,
the hairs around the skin over our brain stems wobbled
as though a breeze from a frozen continent fanned them—
much like the way he fanned the air and caressed
something in the air near the theremin's antenna
We held our breath because we knew he was not
allowed to actually make contact with the theremin

yet we could see how distracted he was
by something we could see he had in mind
but could not approach knowing, we could only be near.
His concentration on what he had in mind was razor-
sharp, so much so we feared he'd forget what he was
doing and touch the theremin which is forbidden
during practice, rehearsals, lessons, and recitals.
We didn't know him for very long although he made
it clear our short time together speeded up his progress
on the theremin. They say it takes someone with even
a modest musical talent thousands of hours
of practice to get close to a melody.
He said he'd already lost two years of his life.
He said he was looking for a wife
but knew there'd be things about himself
he could never tell her and so it was as if
he'd already spoiled a romance he'd only imagined.
The times we heard him play the theremin
we made out just the beginning of what would
no doubt be a difficult career, the bandaged hand
played through the air the way a hand fallen into
its own shape is still surprised enough by what it meets.

# Wartime Photos of My Father

### i

Too far off, too faded: we do not see
The eyes beneath the helmet's shadow, cast
Like a veil against his face, angling vertically
To his arm, which clutches a Wehrmacht prisoner's epaulet.
A hangman's noose on the prisoner's neck. Caption:
*Clowning around, near Rome, 1944.*
I've brought the photo album to the lockup wing.
*Electroshock,* he says, *has made a blur*
*Of all those years.* No telling why he needs
Them back. The ambulance he drove. Palermo
And its DP camp. We sip stale coffee on his bed,
Flipping pages. *This man is someone I don't know,*
He says. A nurse brings coffee, his Thorazine.
*This man,* he says, *this man did not know shame.*

### ii

MI rifles slung on shoulders, backpacks
Spilling over, their climb up the hill to the blasted
Olive tree seems endless. When the German trips,
They kick him back up, the morning bracketed
With distant howitzer fire. A branch that's high
And strong enough is found. They drape the noose,
Abstractedly tighten it. One of *the guys*
At last, my awkward father makes a fist,
Snarling *schnell.* Now, predictably, the German's
Shit himself and mumbles prayers. But it's *a joke*—
They toss the noose to the ground. The August sun
Sharpens detail to a visionary glint
That memory can caress or kill. My father laughs
Along with them. The prisoner puffs a cigarette.

## iii

And so the photograph. The prisoner's made
To smile, though shadows corrode his face, which grins
Like a skull, only mouth and chin revealed,
Disembodied, a jawbone picked from a ruin.
My father is connected to this shadow,
Angling to engulf his face. Does he flinch
Or laugh? Avert his eyes? Or does he smile
His buddies' regulation leer? The olive branches'
Shadows web the ground, complicate these mysteries
With intricate right-angled slashes,
Spoked against the sun's incendiary
Merciless bright. They'll snake their path
Back to camp, the German stumbling, head bowed
As his life comes back to him, a fever dream.

## iv

My father, about whom I have lied. The photo:
Embellished for the sake of—what? A poem,
Though the hospital and war are true, the album.
But the German soldier, frightened to his marrow.
About to be hanged, mostly invention, an added
Dramatic touch to keep you reading on.
(This man, he says, this man did not know shame.)
My father, cruel to no one, cradled
In his silences, in a lime-green gown
By a window latticed with wire. But these
Unvarnished facts were not enough. I face
A man who weeps, his own face still unknown,
And I conjure his past for him. My shame:
Walking past the nurse's station, willing him someone else.

v

The secret missions of a railroad man, gone a week,
Then home a week, each morning sleeping in
To wake alone, his child gone and wife at work.
How did he pass his days? Imagination
Tricks or fails. Do I say he rose at twelve
To sausages and runny eggs? Do I say
He spent his mornings at his woodshop lathes
And saber saws, his wobbling carpentry
Filling the basement and garage? *The Empire Builder*
Is an easier myth. Beneath Montana glaciers,
The engine straining, he leans from the baggage car door.
Surveying his domain, a scene I've written over
And over, into stupid wishful fantasy.
Now the real work: he blinks from mirrors at me.

vi

*Look*, he says, *I'm gone.* The mirror offers steam
Where his face had loomed. He's wrapped in a towel,
Singing Patsy Cline, lathered cheeks, a phantom.
Have we bathed together? And me, how old
Am I? Have I washed his back? No—I won't
Go on with this. Instead, the facts: he lumbers
Down the corridor from his shower. His roommate's
In a manic phase, and writing to some senator
About his *crooked civil servant son*—
*How do you spell betrayal*—E-L, *or* A-L?
I draw the curtains between the beds. Bathrobe open,
My father gives instructions for his burial:
Cremation, no headstone. Will I visit again
Tonight? Will I bring his spare teeth, a comb?

## vii

Words to describe him: stranger, cipher, father.
The son invents a cruelty, a hurt
From years before the son was born—a unit
For measuring distance, the white noise that shimmers
Between our stuttering conversations,
Two men who cannot talk or touch. I wake
Alone in my father's house, and rise to pack
The things he's asked for, the widower's devoted son,
Wrapping dental plates in tissue, framed photographs
Of my mother, pairs of mismatched socks.
They've taken away his shoelaces and belts.
They'll search this bag I bring him, prohibit
Safety razors, sweets. They'll scour away his past.
*Tabula rasa:* the photo album shuts.

## viii

### Military Portrait of My Father
after Rilke

The eyes don't dream, though surely the brow feels
Something remote. Shut lips. Can we penetrate
Such reticence, this sorrow that admits no smile,
Only shadow? On the lap, his medic's helmet,
Scarred and pitted, white oval for the scarlet cross,
Washed-out colors, fingers toying with the strap.
The wrists, which won't stay folded for the pose,
Are milk-white blurs, as if only the hands could grasp
The details for such inwardness. This time, no caption.
And the ringless hands, open or clenched?
Hands and eyes averted, the image beckons,
Then pushes us away. It haunts my desk.
I stare at the glass, my breath against his face. I stare
Until our images dissolve—*shadow into light, son into father.*

# Wander Luís

Ouro Prêto, Brasil


We walk to the top of São Francisco
and huddle under the portico
of the red-tile and soapstone church
while afternoon rain washes away footsteps
of police. "They got my brother
first," you say. "We found his body
in the high grass, bound hand and foot
and blindfolded." *Suicide,*
the uniform at the guard post
shrugged, turning up his soccer game.

You look out past crooked streets
where voices through doorways
chant away the thunder, past
the damp green confusion of hills.
You push dark hair from your eyes,
one hand covers mine
as if tonight your body
could protect me from the story.

Your friends all fled to Chile
in those days: Marcos
in the trunk of the red VW
Regina drove from Rio. Chico Lopes
locked eight months in a closet in Leblon,
lying flat under *Guaraní blankets*
at the Paraguayan border. Marisa,
pregnant, sobbing in a rented room
in Santiago,
                    and you, Wander Luís,

safe in the School of Mines.
The engineering students' *pensão*,
a gallery of blue-shuttered doors,
constant trickle of water in the garden.
"What else can I do?" you ask,
three days from anywhere
on the empty highways
of Minas Gerais, between no life
and no other.

You've learned what's precious
in those hills — diamonds and coal
these towns were named for,
stress-tested metals. And occasionally
a glint of sunlight on a thighbone,
the last white flash of understanding
in the cells. What is the atomic weight
of loss? You know your subject.
*Father, brother, son.* Each name
divided by the blood factor.

"Too many of us live
in doubt's shadow," you say.
Your uncle the graveyard-shift printer,
purple smudges of *samisdat* on his hands
when they came for him.
Your cousin, drilled with M-16 rounds
under the Father of His Country statue.
And you, hitchhiking in Ash Wednesday rain
for the inquest, with drivers
who scarcely knew the language.

How convenient the dead heroes,
after Goulart's and Castelo Branco's madness,
all the blond families friendly

with Stroessner, running the country
like one big *fazênda*, Pôrto Alegre
full of Klaus Barbie connections.

And *Brasil mulato*, laughing and talking
all night, drinking *cachaça* and slave coffee
to forget the parrot perch,
the rubber truncheon, shaved heads
of deportees. Three thousand men
a year who give themselves
to the knife samba, the slow fade
of rain, *favêlas* crumbling on hills
within sight of the Sheratons.

That night, while summer storms
batter the flagstones, I grow
suddenly afraid, ask you to leave.
Harsh words then on your tongue, in my mouth
only sounds that stumble forward
for the border guards, their hands
hard and fast for contraband.

Later, I stand outside your door,
listening to your breath come slow
between the shutters, wondering who
would be left to regret us.
Your one letter months from then,
breathless with dashes and wide-open
vowels — the letter I never answered
for fear you'd follow it
or understand the wanderer's cowardice
that filled my body
with your name.
                              "Next year

I'll be gone," you said.

"London, Santiago, New York . . ."
You slapped your hands in that strange
Brasilian gesture: "*Não se não*" —

*Who knows?* I ask now,
twenty years since corpses floated
under the Mapocho River bridges,
and the rich women of Santiago
parked their cars along the bank
to stare at the dark-skinned ones
among them, and all letters out of Chile
stopped. Twenty years since Marisa
lay down with the child whose name
never reached us, since Chico
slept with a revolver by his pillow
and Marcos finally won his game
of Russian roulette.

                  Twenty years,
Wander Luís, since you sat cross-legged
on a curbstone in the only photo
I have of you, in a white shirt
with its pocketsful of cigarettes
and ballpoints, strumming a *frêvo* rhythm
on your dead brother's guitar,
your eyes half-closed, your face,
like his, never getting any older.

# Hot House

Therapy junkie because
you sucked too
much of your
mother's sweet
nipple, or never
enough, or
it tasted bitter as latex
or dad cried too
often at the table then
hung himself from
the beam of that
Monkey Wards
swing set he'd
erected between
beers one lonely
Saturday. Maybe
you hear his voice over
your shoulder, hot
as galvanized
wheels of a train. Maybe
you seize up all these
years later, when
footsteps threaten your
unlocked door. Maybe
he didn't string
himself up at all, but
600 miles south
of Trinidad doesn't
know your name
anymore than
he knows the woman he calls
*She*, who answers his

chronic questions, the same
She that for fifty
years ironed his handkerchiefs
into rectangles, into the dream
that transports you from
the chaos of plates crashing
until all that's
left are your mother's
worries sprouting a sad
adios and by the time
you look up to that gauzy
blue-lit night,
you're just so
beautifully
squared away.

# Permissions

Ai: "The Calling" from *Dread*. Copyright © 2003 by Ai. Reprinted with permission of W. W. Norton.

Robert Alexander: "For Years My Father" from *White Pine Sucker River* published by New Rivers Press. Copyright © 1993 by Robert Alexander. Reprinted with permission of the author.

Ralph Angel: "The Vigil" from *Twice Removed*. Copyright © 2001 by Ralph Angel. Reprinted with permission of Sarabande Books.

David Baker: "Pulp Fiction" from *Changeable Thunder* published by the University of Arkansas Press. Copyright © 2001 by David Baker. Reprinted with permission of the author.

Marvin Bell: "The Uniform" from *Nightworks: Poems 1962–2000*. Copyright © 2000 by Marvin Bell. Reprinted with permission of Copper Canyon Press.

Elinor Benedict: "At Ease" first appeared in *Zone*. Copyright © 2005 by Elinor Benedict. Reprinted with permission of the author.

Monica Berlin: "Fungus Considered" first appeared in *Flyway*. Copyright © 2003 by Monica Berlin. Reprinted with permission of the author.

Robert Bly: "When My Dead Father Called" from *Eating the Honey of Words: New and Selected Poems* published by HarperCollins. Copyright © 1999 by Robert Bly. Reprinted with permission of the author.

Fleda Brown: "Elvis Decides to Become a Monk" from *The Women Who Loved Elvis All Their Lives*. Copyright © 2004 by Fleda Brown. Reprinted with permission of Carnegie Mellon University Press.

Christopher Buckley: "Catechism of the Sea" copyright © 2005 by Christopher Buckley. Used with permission of the author.

Christopher Bursk: "What a Boy Does Not Say" from *Ovid at Fifteen*. Copyright © 2003 by Christopher Bursk. Reprinted with permission of New Issues Press.

Narda Bush: "Noodling" copyright © 2005 by Narda Bush. Used with permission of the author.

Marcus Cafagña: "Hawthorne Metal, Detroit, 1939" copyright © 2005 by Marcus Cafagña. Used with permission of the author.

Justin Cain: "My Required Tool" copyright © 2005 by Justin Cain. Used with permission of the author.

David Clewell: "Going Wrong in the House of Neptune" from *The Low End of Higher Things*. Copyright © 2003 by David Clewell. Reprinted with permission of the University of Wisconsin Press.

Billy Collins: "Going out for Cigarettes" from *Questions about Angels*. Copyright © 1991 by Billy Collins. Reprinted with permission of the University of Pittsburgh Press.

Gillian Conoley: "The Violence" copyright © 2005 by Gillian Conoley. Used with permission of the author.

# Title Index